D1615082

**The National
Pageant of Wales**

Mr Evan Owen as 'Gerald the Welshman'

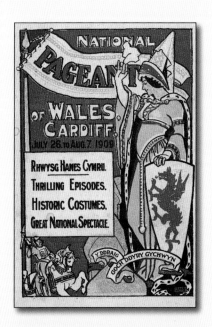

NATIONAL
PAGEANT
OF WALES
CARDIFF.
JULY 26. TO AUG. 7. 1909

RHWYSG HANES CYMRU.
THRILLING EPISODES.
HISTORIC COSTUMES.
GREAT NATIONAL SPECTACLE.

Y DDRAIG   GOCH DDYRY GYCHWYN

The National Pageant of Wales

Hywel Teifi Edwards

Gomer

This book is dedicated to Henry and Frances Jones-Davies, whose love of Wales, as embodied in *Cambria*, inspires and gladdens the hearts of all patriots.

Published in 2009 by
Gomer Press, Llandysul, Ceredigion, SA44 4JL

ISBN 978 1 84851 035 7
A CIP record for this title is available from the British Library.

This book is published with the financial support of the
Welsh Books Council.

Printed and bound in Wales at
Gomer Press, Llandysul, Ceredigion

CONTENTS

ACKNOWLEDGEMENTS   VII

FOREWORD   IX

PREVIEW   1

THE PARKERIAN PAGEANT   13

OWEN RHOSCOMYL (1863-1919)   29

THE GREATEST EVENT IN THE ANNALS OF WALES   87

REVIEW   157

NOTES   201

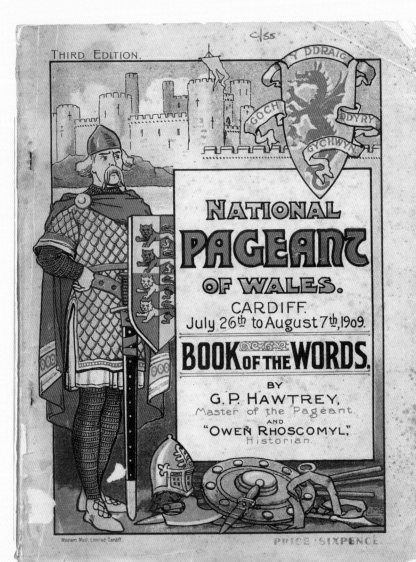

THIRD EDITION.

Y DDRAIG
GOCH DDYRY
GYCHWYN

NATIONAL
PAGEANT
OF WALES.

CARDIFF.
July 26th to August 7th, 1909.

BOOK OF THE WORDS.

BY

G. P. HAWTREY,
Master of the Pageant.

AND

"OWEN RHOSCOMYL,"
Historian.

Western Mail Limited Cardiff.

PRICE SIXPENCE.

ACKNOWLEDGEMENTS

For their assistance in the preparation of this book I wish to thank the staff of the National Library of Wales, Cardiff Council Library Services (especially Katrina Coopey) and Swansea University Library. I also thank *The Western Mail* for permission to include some of J.M. Staniforth's Pageant cartoons and numerous images.

I am indebted to the following for guiding my research in profitable directions and providing me with the most useful materials: Dr Huw Walters, Mr Brynmor Jones, Mr Wil Aaron, Mr Matthew Williams, Miss S. Crawshay, Dr T.F. Holley, Mr Ken Kyffin, Mr Colin Lee and Mr A.R. Allan, University of Liverpool.

For producing such an attractive publication I cannot thank Gomer Press enough, and for her skill in editing and improving the original text I am especially grateful to Francesca Rhydderch. There would, of course, have been no text to prepare for publication had it not been for my wife, Rona, who refused to be deterred by my mystifying manuscript. She qualifies as one of Rhoscomyl's warriors.

MR GODFREY WILLIAMS AS OWEN TUDOR AND THE HONOURABLE
MRS GODFREY WILLIAMS AS QUEEN CATHERINE

FOREWORD

THIS YEAR MARKS the centenary of The National Pageant of Wales, which was staged in Cardiff's Sophia Gardens with the blessing of the fourth Marquiss of Bute. That it fell somewhat short of the overheated expectations of its promoters, leaving a debt of some £2,000, hardly detracts from its interest as the only attempt of its kind, to this day, to present a mass audience with a version of Welsh history from Caradoc's defiance of the Roman Empire to the Act of Union in 1536.

In 1951 J.F. Rees contended that: 'In Wales, history has played a minor part in fostering the idea of nationality.'[1] Twenty years later Professor Prys Morgan maintained that: 'There is no great apron stage, near the audience, as it were; little or no interpretation of history in strip-cartoons, television historical costume drama, and popular historical novels, for Welsh history.'[2] And some thirty years after that, the late Professor Rees Davies had this to say: 'A people's, or a nation's, identity rests not only in its aspiration for the present and the future, but in some measure in the collective memory of a validating past which underpins its identity and sanctions its continuity through time . . . A people without a collective memory of itself, a pantheon of heroes, and the "lieux de mémoire" of a national mythology gradually but inexorably forfeits its identity as a people.'[3]

Viewed in the light of these general assertions by three front-rank Welsh historians The National Pageant assumes a significance scarcely afforded it by our serious-minded historians once that rain-ravaged summer's fortnight at the end of July and the beginning of August, 1909, was over and done with. It wasn't so much that it made a financial loss as that the proper study of Welsh history did not profit by it. It was pageantry, a form of 'showbiz', related – if at a prudent distance – to the Buffalo Bill Show which had wowed the Welsh with its garish vulgarity as much as it had countless other thousands across the world.

Born of the 'affair with pageantry' that unexpectedly came into vogue in England and America during the first quarter of the twentieth century, The National Pageant of Wales attracted a short-lived, press-fomented celebrity. The National Eisteddfod at Abergavenny[4] got up a well-received historical pageant of Gwent in 1913 and Harlech Castle also provided a striking location for an impressive week-long pageant, between 21 and 26 August 1922, that attracted the support of sundry prominent Welsh 'pageanteers', members of the Lloyd George family in particular.[5] But nothing on the scale of 'the great venture' of 1909 was attempted again in Wales.

What follows in this book is essentially a straightforward account of a national enterprise properly seen in the context of a widespread involvement with pageantry that stemmed from Louis Napoleon Parker's innovative Sherborne Pageant in 1905, and best appreciated in the context of a long-frustrated desire to fashion from the history of Wales a story to reinvigorate a small, repressed nation and bring it to the fore as a proven contributor to British and imperial might.

In the event, the story fashioned in English for The National Pageant of Wales by the historian Owen Rhoscomyl, born in Southport to an English father and a Welsh mother, and directed by G.P. Hawtrey, an old Etonian with scant knowledge of Wales, let alone Welsh history, for enactment by a huge cast of some 5,000 players, merits description as a deconstructionist's delight. It invites interpretation and reinterpretation and promises thereby much entertainment.

It certainly deserves to be recollected in 2009. The Pageant's fate, like that of its historian, who died in 1919, was to be forgotten – dismissed as a confection not to the taste of the calloused realists who populated Wales after the Great War. The toppling Celtic cross today marking Rhoscomyl's grave in the old cemetery in Rhyl is symbolic of the depreciation of the nationalistic patriotism that infused his writings – symbolic, too, of the decline of the hero in the course of the iconoclastic century that followed his death. Granted that much of his Victorian baggage – his bloodcurdling royalist, imperialist, militarist and racist enthusiasms – badly needed discarding, he nevertheless merits commemoration for his championing of the Welsh as a people who, once possessed of their history, the story of their struggle as a people to be reckoned with, were capable of making Wales a country not merely of aspiration but of proud achievement.

'How can I shout for Cambria? What is Cambria alone?' wrote H.M. Stanley in a letter to his wife. Rhoscomyl, on the other hand, couldn't shout loud enough for his country's promotion. If he were alive today he should be a contributor to *Cambria*, the one periodical which above all others is dedicated to presenting Wales to the world in all its stunning natural beauty and its enthralling history. Discounted by academic practitioners as a fife-and-drum historian, Rhoscomyl in his day didn't hesitate to draw the firmest of conclusions from the history he studied. He was, psychologically and emotionally, simply not made for the 'on the one hand, on the other' school of historiography. Always on the charge, he wanted to make an impression, and wanted more than anything for the Welsh to see in their history irrefutable proof of their determination to prevail, to survive as a stalwart nation.

In his day Rhoscomyl acted as a whetstone on which his countrymen could hone the blades of their support or opposition. If only we had his like again in 2009 to script a National Pageant (or better still an epic film) to tell the Welsh, who are awaiting yet another referendum to test their readiness for 'a proper parliament', what he told them in the wake of the 'Cymru Fydd' collapse in 1896. Quite simply, as Barack Obama put it on the night of his election victory, when he confronted the difficulties to be overcome, 'Yes, we can.' Rhoscomyl never doubted that the Welsh could be whatever they aspired to be. We will do well to remember him this year as we revisit the Cardiff of 1909 where, for one summer fortnight, as depicted in a *South Wales Daily Post* cartoon, 'chronological chaos' reigned in the city.

THE PAGEANTEERS RETURN FROM SOPHIA GARDENS

NATIONAL PAGEANT *of* WALES

PICTORIAL AND DESCRIPTIVE SOUVENIR

CARDIFF
JULY 26TH TO AUGUST 7TH 1909

Dr James Mullin

PREVIEW

ĪT BEGAN WHEN a short, descriptive article written by a Cardiff worthy, Dr James Mullin, MA, JP, appeared in *The Western Mail*, 5 July 1906. He had just seen a historical pageant in Warwick, a celebratory enactment of incidents in Warwickshire's past that had excited him, as it had thousands of other onlookers, whose initial curiosity soon turned into lively acclaim as the costumed cast of local enthusiasts captured their imagination. Prompted by the fact that the idea originated with a Welshman on the staff of *The Warwick Advertiser*, one Edward Hicks, a former student at Llandovery College, Dr Mullin urged that the possibilities of a similar venture in celebration of Welsh history be explored forthwith. He saw no reason to fear failure: 'We have magnificent settings and surroundings – in fact, every element of success, except the spirit, and that, let us hope, is not absent, but only dormant.'[1]

Cardiff, which was in the full flush of its Edwardian heyday, having achieved city status in 1905, was quick to respond. The Town Clerk, J.L. Wheatley, saw an opportunity to promote Cardiff not only as one of Britain's powerhouses, 'but as one of the most enterprising cities in the Empire'. *The South Wales Daily News* felt sure such a pageant would be a profitable tourist attraction: 'Americans would come in large numbers to Cardiff to witness a Welsh National Pageant, and it would do much to advertise Wales in America.'[2] But over and above any commercial benefits that could accrue, it was felt that a pageant such as Dr Mullin visualized would infuse the nation with a charge of patriotic fervour and would boost a spirit of self-assertion. A Wales apprised of its former renown, its resolve stiffened by a dramatic presentation of the splendour of its own story, would be better fitted to play a praiseworthy part in Great Britain's ongoing imperial saga. The American Consul in Cardiff, Mr D. Webster Williams, quoting the example of the 'Old Home Day' in New Hampshire 'as an instance of what historical pageantry was capable of in stimulating love of home and country', saw no reason to fear a cheapening of cultural import by an intrusive profit motive. But true to the Cymrodorion ethic, Councillor J.T. Richards argued for a pageant that would issue in something considerably more improving than a short-lived entertainment. It should bear fruit in a standard history book for use in schools throughout Wales.[3]

On his return from Warwick, Dr Mullin chanced to meet with Mr Isaac Vaughan Evans, Cardiff's Chief Inspector of Schools, who at the time was the secretary of the Cymrodorion Society. He broached the subject of a National Pageant and the likelihood of the Cymrodorion taking the lead in exploring the possibilities. Quick to respond, Evans invited him to give the Society a lecture on pageantry and on what he had seen in Warwick in particular. It proved to be a decisive step. At its meeting on 17 July 1906, the Cymrodorion Society, founded in 1885 and with a membership of 1,250 in 1909 that included some of the city's most influential Welshmen, pressed the Lord Mayor to convene a public meeting to gauge the level of support for such an undertaking.[4]

The Western Mail and *The South Wales Daily News* proceeded to whip up enthusiasm by making large claims for Welsh patriotism: 'No race is more alive to the demands of patriotism. When Wales is named, the Welshman thrills with pride. It is not his fault if the nation is not in

Under Dewi's Patronage.

DEWI SANT : Jawch, my gel ! What is on you ? Are you gone off your head, or what is the matter ?

DAME WALES : Oh, no, Dewi bachan ! But come in, look you, an' let me tell you all about it. Indeed, now, you will be delighted, for I am preparing for a National Pageant. I propose to represent in proper costumes, and out in the open air, look you, past incidents in my history. What do you think of that, Dewi ?

DEWI SANT : Famous, my gel, famous ! I shall be there to see it.

(A Staniforth cartoon)

the van.' For three years, the wheels of hype would turn steadily in Cardiff, before beginning to spin furiously as the summer of 1909 drew nearer. On 21 September 1906, at a public meeting in the Town Hall convened by the city's first Lord Mayor, Alderman Robert Hughes, a native of Llanegryn in Meirionneth, a committee was appointed 'pro tem' to draw up draft plans for a National Pageant to be held in 1908. It was composed of the current Archdruid of Wales – the Reverend Evan Rees (Dyfed), Alderman Edward Thomas (Cochfarf), Mr T.H. Thomas (Arlunydd Pen-y-garn), Dr James Mullin, Councillor J.T. Richards, Mr S.W. Allen and Mr J. Austin Jenkins, BA, together with the Lord Mayor and Mr Isaac Vaughan Evans as 'ex officio' members,

Mr Isaac Vaughan Evans

Evans acting as secretary 'pro tem'. It would be their responsibility to bring their plans to the attention of as wide a selection of respondents as possible, at home and abroad, so as to preclude the danger of adverse criticism on the grounds of inadequate consultation and preparation should the venture fail.[5]

For the next two years this Cymrodorion-driven committee 'did excellent spade-work in popularizing the idea'. There was a particular need to explore the likely response of some of the leading figures in Welsh life, chief among them the representatives of the country's historic families. After the meeting on 21 September 1906, Mr J. Austin Jenkins, BA, the Registrar of Cardiff University College, together with Mr S.W. Allen, 'drafted a sketch of the historical episodes which might be acted'. It was subsequently included in the first circular sent out by Mr Isaac Vaughan Evans 'to leading men and women in Wales and Monmouthshire asking for their support to the Pageant', signalling the launch of a plan of action which would result in *The Western Mail* emphasizing later on that 'the remarkable rapidity and ease with which the Pageant was eventually organised is in a large measure due to the preliminary proceedings on the part of the Cymmrodorion'. On Friday afternoon, 23 July 1909, due recognition of the Society's role in 'the great venture' was given by the Marchioness of Bute when, of nearly a thousand guests attending her garden party in the Castle grounds, by far the largest group was made up of Cymrodorion zealots.[6]

The South Wales Daily News was eager to enthuse its readers. There was no subject 'more profitably fascinating' than history, as the pageant was bound to demonstrate:

The glorious history of the Principality set forth as an object lesson could not fail to instil into the minds of the young the higher patriotism that in their forefathers kept Wales a distinct and national unity and made her a more powerful factor in Imperial progress because she was true to herself.[7]

F.R. Benson, the celebrated Shakespearian actor-manager who was in Cardiff during September 1906 to play 'Hamlet' at the Royal Theatre, was more than happy to orate in support of the projected pageant. His company had in 1898 marked the 500th anniversary of Richard II's progress to Flint Castle, and as a result he had become a confirmed pageant-lover, so much so that in 1907 he staged pageants in Romsey and on the Isle of Wight. If the Welsh could secure Cardiff Castle as the focus for their presentation of an eventful narrative fashioned from the wealth of materials to hand, a narrative highlighting the spiritual every bit as much as the material content of their past, they would have a hit for sure: 'What a country and what a history for a picturesque object-lesson to the present generation . . . Wales . . . could present an unparalleled pageant.'[8]

Three years would elapse before the tidal Celtic enthusiasm, set in motion by Dr Mullin's prompting in a city already astir with civic advance, found a clear channel. It was quickly realized in 1906 that a National Pageant, no matter how instant its romantic appeal, needed money, planning and determination in the face of many obstacles before it could assume form and purpose. The venture seemed stalled when the Lord Mayor of Oxford, following a successful pageant performed in his city in 1907, saw fit to dissuade Cardiff from taking up a challenge for which it appeared poorly equipped. Dr James Mullin responded in *The Western Mail*, 23 July 1908, insisting: 'The scheme is not dead, but exists in a state of suspended animation, and the enthusiasm necessary to arouse it is gathering force every day.' In 1906, the city's energies had been fittingly exhausted in preparing an unbuttoned Welsh welcome for a visit by King Edward VII. But now there was a determination to accelerate progress with a view to staging a pageant that would not only entertain the common people, but make the whole nation 'more self-respecting than hitherto, and more likely to live up to the standard of ancestral merit'.[9]

It was as late as February 1909 when preparations really got under way. An all-male executive committee, numbering thirty-nine members chaired by the Lord Mayor, Alderman Lewis Morgan, had by then secured a guarantee fund amounting to £2,800. As many as nine sub-committees were formed – Finance, Press and Advertising, Property and Costumes, Music, Performers, Grand Stand, Entertainments, Railway and Steamboats, and Horses – not a single one of which was chaired by a woman. Mr A.W. Swash and Mr J. Allcock were appointed Secretary and Treasurer respectively, and the crucial posts of Pageant-Master, and Historian cum Deputy Pageant-Master, were entrusted to

THE MARQUISS OF BUTE

THE MARCHIONESS OF BUTE

George P. Hawtrey, MA, and Captain Arthur Owen Vaughan (Owen Rhoscomyl), of whom there will be more to say anon. For six frenetic months, from February to July 1909, there was a concerted effort to create a National Pageant worthy of the splendid castle-dominated location in Sophia Gardens which the readily supportive Marquiss of Bute made available.[10]

There, from 26 July to 7 August, Cardiff would revel in a bravura enactment of Welsh history, ranging from Caradoc's defiance of imperial Rome circa 50 BC to the Act of Union between England and Wales in 1536. Following the lead given by the Butes – the Marchioness consented to represent 'Dame Wales' – members of some of the historic families of Wales threw their patrician weight behind the venture, foremost among them Lord Tredegar, who came not only as a resolute Welshman proud of his Morgan antecedents, but as a 'bona fide' British hero who had survived the murderously mad 'Charge of the Light Brigade' in the Crimea in 1854. He would be Owain Glyndŵr:

> Our chief is a warrior brave and bold,
> A lord of Old Tredegar;
> One of that wonderful Brigade
> That made the world to shudder:
> His name will live in every land
> For ever and for ever.

Members of the illustrious Mostyn family in Flintshire took part, as did the Scudamores of Kentchurch Court, the Bassetts of Beaupre, the various Williams families of Aberpergwm, Miskin Manor and St Donat's Castle, the Joneses of Fonmon Castle, the Lewises of Greenmeadow, the Crawshays of Dimlands, the Stuarts of Dinas Powys – in short, Cardiff's National Pageant could boast of upper-class participants whose historical associations, combined with latter-day landed and industrial wealth, would doubtless authenticate the enterprise and invest it with 'éclat'.[11]

Not to be sidelined by their betters, civic dignitaries, city councillors, council officers and various other public servants were also keen to take leading parts. The Lord Mayor assumed the role of Hywel Dda; Mr Isaac Vaughan Evans took to 'Llywelyn Olav'; Mr Ifano Jones, the City Librarian, played Merlin the Wizard; Captain Lindsay, the Chief Constable of Glamorgan who would lead his force against the striking Rhondda miners in 1910, threatingly took the part of the predatory 'Chief Ruffian' whose evil designs on the fair maids of the Tywi Valley were thwarted by Hywel Dda.[12]

Schoolteachers of both sexes, together with hundreds of their pupils, mostly girls disporting themselves as fairies, took to pageantry with unbounded enthusiasm, and for the storming of Cardiff Castle by Ivor Bach's men in 1178, as many as five hundred rugby players (it was said) were recruited by W.T. Morgan, the president of Cardiff Rugby Club, some of them, such as Charlie Arthur, Alex Bland, W.M.

Douglas, P.C. Brice, R.T. Gabe, Reggie Gibbs, J. Powell and J.L. Williams were stars of their day, R.T. Gabe, for instance, having excelled at centre in the epochal victory against the All Blacks in 1905 and the securing of the first Grand Slam in 1908. Indeed, in the jubilation that followed the close of The National Pageant an exultant Lord Mayor put things in their proper perspective: 'We have beaten the world at football, and now we have beaten the world, also, at pageantry. I thank you.' (W.T. Morgan's reward was the part of Henry VIII in the final interlude scene.) The success achieved in Sophia Gardens in 1909 was seen to equal the rugby triumphs of 1905 and 1908 as proof

W.T. MORGAN,
PRESIDENT OF CARDIFF RFC

of the stalwart character of the Welsh nation. Such feats surely merited positive recognition outside the world of Wales, recognition of a kind the Welsh had long craved in their history – and still do crave a century after Lord Mayor Lewis Morgan's shout of self-congratulation.[13]

In a cast of some 5,000 performers, the better part of a thousand of them were fairies who helped form the living map of Wales that made the final scene of the pageant so memorable. Some 40,000 pieces of costume were designed by J.M. Staniforth (1863-1921), *The Western Mail*'s inspired cartoonist who had given the nation 'Dame Wales', and his designs were fashioned into costumes by a small army of 800 'lady workers' overseen by twenty-five superintendents, chief among them Mrs T. Snead Davies, who week after week put in three shifts a day in a building in Wharton Street lent gratis by the munificent James

J.M. STANIFORTH

Howell and known temporarily as 'Pageant House'. And in Sophia Gardens, where the great drama was to unfold, a makeshift grandstand was erected to seat 7,500 spectators, with another 17,000 seated in stands provided by Cardiff Rugby Football Club. In the grandstand a mixed choir of 250 voices (the women dressed in Lady Llanover Welsh costume) sang, as the Pageant dictated, to the accompaniment of the Band of the Royal Marines (Portsmouth Division), conducted by Lieutenant G. Miller, MVO, and for the evening performances floodlights intensified the sense of romance, making the various scenes appear 'more truly Celtic' for Christopher Williams, the Maesteg-born artist.[14]

Come 26 July, Cardiff was about to abandon itself to a fortnight of 'chronological chaos'. All agog, 'bright young things' asked one another 'Are you going to "padge"?', and the worthies who constituted the executive committee, having failed to secure the presence of a royal personage despite advertising the attractions of hunters, hounds and fair ladies, took comfort in a visit willingly undertaken by the Lord Mayor of London – the Cornishman, Sir George Wyatt Truscott. Alderman Edward Thomas (Cochfarf), born a farmer's son near Maesteg and a fervent Welshman who served Cardiff well as councillor, JP and its Mayor in 1902, would find reason to rejoice in the sight of 'a democracy of patriots' on the Pageant field, an intermingling of people where 'a patrician does not shun the horny-handed wealth-producer, and the so-called "lower classes" demonstrate that they possess as much dignity of mien and speech as the "higher classes"'. Councillor Edward Nicholl would buy stand tickets for 350 workhouse inmates, and David Davies, MP, as Captain of the Llandinam and Llanidloes contingent, would pay for 550 members of the Royal Welsh Fusiliers (7th Battalion), encamped at Abergavenny, to visit the Pageant in a train especially hired for the occasion. Led by Colonel Sir Lenox Napier, their exemplary conduct would win them plaudits as they marched back to the station, singing 'How can I bear to leave thee?' in strident appreciation of what they had witnessed. Even the phlegmatic

MRS T. SNEAD DAVIES, 'CAPTAIN' OF THE LADY WORKERS

Australian cricket team who had come to play and defeat a South Wales XI at the Arms Park during the August Bank Holiday would adjudge the Pageant 'a beaut' after attending an evening performance, together with the home side, as guests of the Lord Mayor.[15]

What follows in this account will place The National Pageant of Wales in the context of 'the affair with pageantry' that blossomed in England between 1905 and 1909, and will underline its significance as a banner-waving historical narrative for an untutored audience long adrift from 'its own story'. A number of contemporary Welsh commentators were anxious to convince themselves that the Pageant could change what they held had been for too long, both within and without the country, a fixed, debilitating view of 'the worthiness of

MAKING COSTUMES IN 'PAGEANT HOUSE'

Wales'. The nation's long dormant historical awareness was in need of a regenerative shock and where better to administer it than in Cardiff, the newly-born city, the metropolis that in 1909 pulsed with 'New World' energy. A successful National Pageant staged there would surely hasten the emergence of a self-belief without which all talk of nation-building amounted to nothing.

THE PARKERIAN PAGEANT

R JAMES MULLIN'S account of the Warwick Pageant was unstinting in its praise of the 2,000 performers who, for thirteen months, had prepared assiduously for their triumph. He was equally appreciative of the audience, especially the fashionably attired ladies whose predominance lent an irresistible charm to the occasion, and his description of the setting made it clear that it was central to the 'magnificence' of the pageant:

> The arena and amphitheatre cover seven acres in the grounds of
> Warwick Castle, and consist of green sward, bounded on the left
> by the Avon, and on the right by majestic trees – oaks, elms,
> chestnuts, and cedars. Away in the background there is a rising
> landscape densely wooded, and further in front some fine beech
> trees. In addition to the trees and the river, on either side there
> is a dense shrubbery, which served as wings whence the actors
> had their entrances and exits. The grandstand was semi-circular
> in shape, and well roofed, effectually protecting against sun and
> rain.[1]

THE WARWICK PAGEANT:
THE CAST DISBANDS

It was a setting fit for entrancing performances of Shakespeare's *A Midsummer Night's Dream* or *As You Like It*.

What was conjured up there in eleven 'episodes' was some 2,000 years of Warwick's history 'interwoven with the general history of England'. The Pageant actually commemorated 'the one thousandth anniversary of the conquest of Mercia, and the overthrow of Paganism therein, by Ethelfreda, Lady of the Mercians 906 AD'. Listing the eleven 'episodes' in the following order –

1. The Dawn of Christianity in Britain
2. How 'The Bear and Ragged Staff' became the badge of the Earls of Warwick
3. Ethelfreda, the daughter of Alfred, AD 906
4. The story of Guy of Warwick and his love for fair Phyllis
5. The return of Roger de Newburgh, Earl of Warwick, from a Crusade; date, 1123
6. The trial of Piers Gaveston – the act of wild justice which led up to the Wars of the Roses
7. Warwick, the maker and unmaker of Kings
8. Granting of a charter to the town of Warwick, 1546
9. Proclamation of Lady Jane Grey as Queen in Warwick, 1563
10. Queen Elizabeth's visit to Warwick, 1572
11. The great fire that burned down Warwick in 1694

Dr Mullin summed up the impressions left by their enactment as 'minglings of delight and wonder'. The whole Pageant reflected great credit on the local populace whose involvement from the beginning had been total, including 300 ladies who made 1,400 costumes with their own hands, the Mayor who gave 100 guineas to open a guarantee fund, and the Earl of Warwick who promised the use of the castle grounds. It was in all respects a people's venture, calculated to engender pride in past glories and a determination 'to hand them down untarnished and undiminished'.[2]

Having made clear the importance of Edward Hicks, both as

prompter of the undertaking and tireless secretary of the executive committee whose responsibility it was to ensure success, Dr James Mullin also noted that 'Mr Louis Parker, the well-known playwright and organiser of the Sherborne pageant, was secured for the book of words, and the general management.'[3] By 1909 Parker's significance as the trigger and promoter of 'the affair with pageantry' during the first decade of the twentieth century was widely recognized, his particular kind of pageant having first imprinted itself on the public imagination in Sherborne in 1905. By the following summer it was assuming the features of a phenomenon.

Born in 1852 at Luc-sur-Mer in Calvados, Normandy, to an English mother, Elizabeth Moray, and an American father, Charles Albert Parker, he was christened Louis Napoleon Parker (1852-1944). His father was a compulsive roamer and away from home when his son was born. The mother, not knowing what name to give him, sought the advice of a French neighbour who idolized Louis Napoleon, and that settled the matter. A childhood spent in several European countries saw him grow up fluent in Italian, French and German, but he was to blossom as a musician, and his parents sent him, at the age of seventeen, to study at the Royal Academy of Music in London. There, under Sir William Sterndale Bennett's tuition, he distinguished himself as singer, pianist and organist, his talents taking him to the famous Sherborne School in Dorset in 1873, where he was to assume the post of director of music and stay until 1892 when his defective hearing thwarted his ambitions as a musician.

From Sherborne he turned to London and redirected his creative energies towards the theatre. A fervent Wagnerian – he was among the earliest members of the original Wagner Society – he was to take to the 'unsettling' plays of Ibsen, Maeterlinck and Shaw with equal passion, and over many years spent as a productive playwright and translator of European drama, he would win for himself a reputation as an out-and-out man of the theatre, a radical spirit held in high regard by many of the foremost dramatists of his age.[4]

When, in 1905, the people of Sherborne proposed to celebrate the 1200th anniversary of 'the town, the bishopric and the school' with a folk play to be performed in the grounds of Sherborne Castle, they turned to Louis Napoleon Parker for assistance. What resulted was a historical pageant composed of eleven 'episodes', illustrating the town's history from 705 AD to 1593 – a pageant of a kind that bore little resemblance to the masques and pageants of medieval, Tudor and Stuart England – to be followed by another five in Warwick (1906), Bury St Edmunds (1907), Dover (1908), Colchester (1909) and York (1909). They would make Parker's name a byword for a newfangled display of historical romanticism suffused with English patriotism – Parker demonstrating the strength of his own affiliation by becoming a British subject shortly before the Great War began in 1914.[5]

Robert Withington, in his work on *English Pageantry*, noted the totally unexpected success of the Sherborne pageant. Parker, as pageant-master, was feeling his way and had to contend with a liberal measure of ridicule as he prepared his amateur cast of 900 to perform, convincingly, a form of dramatic art that could draw on no approximate supportive tradition. There seemed little prospect of an audience, let alone an enthusiastic audience to fill a grandstand, until a dress rehearsal took place ten days before the first official performance. Rousing reports by a couple of journalists triggered an astonishing response which brought some 50,000 people in all to Sherborne to witness seven performances of Parker's pageant. In Withington's words, 'All England took fire', and was to remain on fire throughout the Edwardian period and beyond, as Parker's brand of pageantry, which to all intents and purposes constituted a new genre, became all the rage, sweeping 'the United States from end to end; from Boston to California, from Quebec to New Orleans'.[6]

By 1909 Parker had crystallized what were for him the defining features of his creation. Its 'raison d'être' was clear:

A Pageant is a Festival of Thanksgiving, in which a great city or a little hamlet celebrates its glorious past, its prosperous present, and its hopes and aspirations for the future. It is a commemoration of Local Worthies. It is also a great Festival of Brotherhood; in which all distinctions of whatever kind are sunk in a common effort. It is, therefore, entirely undenominational and non-political. It calls together all the scattered kindred from all parts of the world. It reminds the old of the history of their home, and shows the young what treasures are in their keeping. It is the great incentive to the right kind of patriotism: love of hearth; love of town; love of country; love of England.[7]

Based on 'authentic history', while embracing folklore and picturesque tradition, it told its story in dramatic form, 'in spoken dialogue: in song and in dance where dance and song are admissible'. It could include every form of drama, 'tragedy, comedy, even farce'.

As for the participants or, to use the term favoured by Parker, 'the executants', they had to include every class of the community of both sexes:

> . . . peers and ploughboys; dignitaries of the church and all the clergy; ministers of every denomination; young men and maidens; old men and children; the beautiful and the less beautiful; youth is no hindrance, and age no bar; nobody is too good to be in a Pageant and almost everybody is good enough . . . A Pageant is absolutely democratic. That is one of its many merits.[8]

And just as important as its democratic character would be its freedom from pecuniary interests. Parker had to insist

LOUIS NAPOLEON PARKER

'with all possible emphasis' that: 'A Pageant must never be undertaken with a view to making money.' It had to be worth doing for itself: 'If it be not worth that, it is worth nothing, and had much better be left undone.'[9]

One can only conclude that pageantry, as conceived by Louis Napoleon Parker, was meant to be as spiritually uplifting as it was educative and edifying. He viewed the past as a romanticist who feared that all romance was soon to perish before the grinding advance of modernity: 'This modernising spirit which destroys all loveliness and has no loveliness of its own to put in its place, is the negation of poetry, the negation of romance . . . this is just precisely the kind of spirit which a properly organised and properly conducted pageant is designed to kill.' For him, drama rooted in folk play would be the motor of his pageantry, and he would have concurred with William Orr's view that: 'The factors essential to true pageantry are the use of the costumes and practices of other days and the representation of important events in history as expressions of the manifold activities and aspirations of the human soul.'[10]

In his 'Foreword' to the *Book of the York Pageant* (1909), Parker was at pains to point up the national dimension of the new form of dramatic art he had first brought before the public in 1905. Essentially local and amateur in respect of script content and players, its patriotic reach, nevertheless, could encompass the nation. The York Pageant, which over three months drew an audience of half a million people, spanned English history from 800 BC to the Revolution of 1688. It was Parker's last undertaking as pageant-master in England and he had no doubts about the grandeur of what he had achieved: 'Drama lifting our souls to God, and our hearts to the King – is not that National Drama?'[11] The answer, for him, could only be a resounding 'Yes'.

Completely won over, *The Times* in July 1909 applauded Parker's wizardry: 'There must have been a gap in the public imagination waiting to be filled by this particular branch of antiquarianism in our antiquarian age; but not to every one is it given to fill such gaps with the fortune and foresight shown by Mr Parker.' The York Pageant cost, in all, £13,677-9-2 to produce and perform, but the takings amounted to £14,439-18-9, leaving a profit of £762-9-7. Parker's trenchant anti-commercialism notwithstanding, a profit-making pageant was always a desirable outcome in the eyes of its promoters. Tourist and pecuniary interests proved as impossible to ignore in the kingdom of historical pageantry as in the world at large.[12]

Remarking on the structure of the York Pageant, *The Times* noted: 'As usual, Mr Parker fits a period into an "episode" and within the limits of each episode lets century run into century with scarcely a pause, while between the episodes the narrative chorus supplies and comments on the connecting links.' The episode, which from the outset was the governing unit in the Parkerian pageant, functioned as an extended dramatization of some significant event or development in the history of a particular locality, region or country. It was to be 'complete in itself', performed by 'a separate and independent cast' and not play for more than a quarter of an hour 'save under very exceptional circumstances'. Each episode was supported by a cluster of brief 'interludes', and the whole pageant progressed in episodic fashion to the conclusion of its narrative. The various episodes, each of which had its own story to tell, were interlinked by the central idea that the pageant was meant to illustrate, and its performance demanded of the pageant-master a theatrical know-how that meshed the skills involved in the deployment of procession, drama, music and dance to create, as was intended, a spellbinding spectacle. To work its magic the Parkerian pageant had to be truly spectacular.[13]

That such a seemingly rudimentary form of dramatic art proved so popular during the opening decades of the twentieth century might strike us as strange. Parker noted that between 1905-09 he 'had invitations from thirty-five important towns; from the American Boston; from Cape Town; and (of all places in the world!) from Mentone.' He also noted that during the Great War pageants featured often among as many as eighty-five War Fund Entertainments, the 'Pageant of

Freedom' especially enjoying 'quite a run'. However rudimentary, there is no denying its effectiveness in its day as a medium for popularizing history, a one-dimensional history admittedly, by presenting 'truths' embedded in images that were very easy on the romantic eye. For Robert Withington, writing at the time of the Great War, modern pageants bore 'much the same relation to us that the chronicle-play bore to the Elizabethan audience', and as he considered 'historical exposition' to be the 'soul of Parkerian pageant', the dialogue, which of necessity had to be pared down for 'al fresco' performances, was important. What was seen by the eye needed confirming with brief, apt, audible speech. The appeal of the historical pageant to the early twentieth-century audience is not so difficult to understand, given the instant and ongoing popularity of the historical film which superseded it. Hollywood's 'stupendous spectaculars' were to prove irresistible. The film industry, however, did not eliminate pageantry, it rather subsumed it, and in so doing extended time and again the pageant's celebratory portrayal of patriotism in action.[14]

In 1909, Louis Napoleon Parker's involvement as pageant-master in Colchester and York meant that Cardiff would have to look elsewhere for someone to oversee the preparations and direct the actual performances of The National Pageant of Wales. On 1 February 1909, the selection committee that had been formed to appoint a fitting person to fulfil what was a crucial role recommended 'that Mr G.P. Hawtrey, M.A., be appointed Master of the Pageant on the grounds of scholarship and experience of theatrical matters, and as having acted in a similar capacity at the Cheltenham pageant, when a profit of £1,100 was realised'. Parker's unworldly attitude to money-making was not about to dominate thinking in Edwardian Cardiff, where the aim was to create a pageant that would be profitable in all respects.[15]

George Procter Hawtrey (1847-1910), the son of the Reverend John William Hawtrey, headmaster of Alden House School in Slough, had been educated at Eton and Pembroke College, Oxford. He did not follow in his father's footsteps, opting instead for a career as actor, playwright and pageant-master. His two brothers, William and Charles, were also actors, and it is no surprise, given Hawtrey's superior educational background, work in the theatre and striking success as 'master' of the Gloucestershire Historical Pageant at Cheltenham in 1908, that the executive committee in Cardiff rejoiced in his appointment. After all, where in their drama-starved, theatre-neglected homeland could they hope to find someone as impressively accoutred as Hawtrey for the task in hand – the staging of a National Historical Pageant – an enterprise never before attempted in Wales.[16]

Needless to say, Hawtrey inevitably bore the imprint of Parker's thinking, as Parker had formed a favourable impression of him during the Warwick Pageant when Hawtrey had joined him in the crow's-nest and capitalized on his instruction. But Hawtrey was prepared to disagree with him on certain points. He argued, for instance, that Parker's insistence on producing pageants that owed their existence strictly to voluntary local labour could be counterproductive. In a letter to the

G.P. HAWTREY, PAGEANT-MASTER

Cheltenham committee in 1908, he maintained that attendances at rehearsals had been low because of the requirement that the players should buy their own costumes. As many as 671 of the total cast had 'not attended a single rehearsal', and Hawtrey protested that it was wrong to try making money out of them: 'We are conferring no benefit on the town by taking the shillings of working girls, and sending the money away to London, whence not a penny will ever return.'[17]

To boost his application for the pageant-master's post in Cardiff, he sent the executive committee a forty-four page document detailing his thoughts on the proper organization of a pageant, and assuring them that should he be appointed he was prepared to undertake the entire management. He would have learned from Parker that as pageant-master he would be 'ultimately responsible for everything', and that to get things done exactly as he wanted he would have to 'exercise absolute autocracy; an autocracy tempered by commonsense'. By the time he published his autobiography, *Several of My Lives*, in 1928, Parker, if asked 'to indicate the ideal Master of the Pageant' would have 'unhesitatingly' pointed to Signor Benito Mussolini![18]

Among the points he made in his submission, the following reveal how he proposed to secure a successful outcome to the Cardiff venture. First and foremost, it was not in respect of its money-making potential, but rather in its worth as a significantly edifying cultural event, that a pageant should be prized. The pageant-master should choose his assistants wisely and know enough to be sure that everything was being done efficiently. The site should be so located as not to permit 'free views' of the performance. Players, whether rich or poor, should not be pressed to pay for their costumes. As it could sometimes be difficult to enlist sufficient numbers of male participants, it was important to remember how Parker had persuaded shops to close for the afternoon performances of his pageants. The price of admission should be set at a shilling for the majority of seats or the common people would stay away – as they had done in 1908 when admission to the London Olympic Games proved prohibitive. Advertising had to be well directed: 'After the Welsh, the most likely fish to angle for are American and Colonial visitors.' For a pageant-master to direct a notable performance, the telephone was an indispensable aid: 'From this point [a small box atop of the grandstand] he communicates by telephone with the various positions where the performers are drawn up and gives them the order to make their entrances.' And finally, having witnessed the nuisance caused by the sale of refreshments during the actual performance at Cheltenham, such a disruptive practice should not be tolerated in Cardiff. (He

A POSTCARD PROMOTING THE NATIONAL PAGEANT OF WALES

should have lived to curse the bladdering confusion of rugby's beer-swillers at the Millennium Stadium nowadays.)[19]

There is no doubt that the executive committee in Cardiff had reason to thank their good fortune in acquiring Hawtrey's services. As a practical man of the theatre, sufficiently knowledgeable and experienced to act as 'producer-director,' he was a convincing figure. And he had grasped the significance of what they were about: 'This is a National, not a local, Pageant; not a Pageant of Cardiff, but a Pageant of Wales. It deals with a history which is very little known, although the materials for it exist in masses.' He was at pains from the outset to make clear his awareness that 'to be associated with this, the first National Pageant, is a high privilege and a great responsibility, both of which facts I fully appreciate.' His attitude towards the task, as evinced in such words, could only have struck his Welsh employers as commendable. But there was a problem to overcome. Quite simply, Hawtrey knew no Welsh history, or as he put it with splendid Etonian 'élan', his knowledge of Welsh history 'was not so extensive as to cause me any embarrassment'. He was in no position to script a Pageant of Wales.[20]

The problem was resolved when, on 4 February 1909, one of the most explosive characters ever to indulge an interest in Welsh history was interviewed in Cardiff for the post of 'Historian and Deputy Pageant-Master' by the selection committee, with Hawtrey in attendance. Under his authorial name, Owen Rhoscomyl, he came on the wings of a sweeping recommendation from Sir Thomas Marchant Williams, editor of *The Nationalist* (1907-12), a Welsh task force in the guise of a periodical for which Rhoscomyl made many a cavalry charge. 'He is', said Sir Marchant of him, 'saturated with knowledge of every phase of Welsh history, and is fully alive to the deep significance and the stirring romance of some of its episodes.' His opinion was subsequently endorsed in E.A. Morphy's hyperbolic *Pictorial and Descriptive Souvenir of the National Pageant of Wales*, where Rhoscomyl was presented as 'probably the deepest and ablest scholar of Welsh history now living'. He was, of course, appointed and the work of shaping a 'Story of Wales' to excite the greatest interest and ignite a passionate involvement was entrusted to a man fit to be a war lord in another existence. The ultimate success of a National Pageant would rest on his narrative and Hawtrey's staging of it.[21]

THE IRASCIBLE
SIR MARCHANT WILLIAMS

Owen Rhoscomyl, aka Arthur Owen Vaughan

OWEN RHOSCOMYL (1863-1919)

BORN IN SOUTHPORT, 6 September 1863, to a Welsh mother and an English father, and christened Robert Scourfield Mills, Owen Rhoscomyl was to live a life of improbable derring-do until cancer did for him in a London nursing home on 15 October 1919. Brought back to Wales, he was buried with full military honours in Rhyl on 20 October. His funeral service was conducted in Welsh, his coffin draped in the Red Dragon and three hundred soldiers from the camp at nearby Kinmel fired three salvos above the grave of 'Lt-Col A.O. Vaughan, DSO, DCM, OBE'. *The Western Mail* gave Rhoscomyl's death great prominence, mourning the loss of 'a man of extraordinary parts' whose dynamism had stamped his imprint on the Welsh imagination, and it moved his friend, J. Glyn Davies, poet and Professor of Celtic at Liverpool University, to say that: 'He was the only thorough paced, out-and-out Welsh patriot I have ever met.'[1]

J. GLYN DAVIES

Rhoscomyl still awaits his biographer – a fact that reflects the difficulty of recreating his life when so little is known about long periods of it. Among his papers in the National Library of Wales there is a letter written by his daughter, Olwen Vaughan, to his niece, his sister Ada's daughter, Dorothy Stott, on 24 March 1969, in which she explains how the solicitor who notified her of her mother's death in 1927 'suggested that I burn the accumulation of father's correspondence and papers when I asked him how I should dispose of them, and this I did to my lasting regret'. We share her regret and curse the 'advice' of the aforementioned benighted solicitor in like measure, for it surely deprived us of essential information about Rhoscomyl's family background which went unrecorded by his associates. On his death (Sir) O.M. Edwards, for instance, stated that he had known Rhoscomyl well since 1904 and had shared many of his secrets, but he had never properly understood who his family were *'yn ôl y cnawd'* (in the flesh).[2]

This chapter is primarily concerned with the Rhoscomyl approach to Welsh history that would shape the story told in The National Pageant of Wales. His life is a subject for an extended study, but given the force of his extraordinary persona it is as well to outline certain passages in his own story before introducing the historian. Drawing on information in the Owen Rhoscomyl Papers in the National Library of Wales, on his various writings for newspapers and periodicals, on his autobiographical novels – *Old Fireproof* (1906), *A Scout's Story* (1908) and *Lone Tree Lode* (1913) – and on the tributes of his admirers in the press, it is hoped to convey something of the excitement that pervaded his life from the beginning and made his arrival on the Welsh scene late in the Victorian era as startling as a shell-burst. It was his boast, let us not forget, that: 'My life has been spent from boyhood in wandering, stockriding, prospecting, hunting, scouting, and fighting wherever fighting was to be had', and recognizing that he saw himself as a character far better fitted for novelistic treatment than conventional Victorian autobiography, one can only applaud his literary discrimination. He was made for the wide, open spaces and the vast reaches of the imperial adventure story. *The Welsh Outlook* did well in its obituary notice to recognize him as more Elizabethan than modern man, an adventurer who 'never veiled his flag before the common-place', who would have been 'sworn brother with those old adventurers who broke gaily into seas that no man's eye had ever before beheld'. The obituarist's claim that: 'Those who stood with Cortes, "silent upon a peak in Darien," were men whom Rhoscomyl would understand and who would, in turn, understand Rhoscomyl', is particularly apt.[3]

On 16 October 1863 Robert Mills, whose family roots were in Rochdale, died as a result of an industrial accident little more than a month after the birth of his son, Robert Scourfield Mills, aka Arthur Owen Vaughan, aka Owen Rhoscomyl. Rhoscomyl's mother, Jane Ann, had her roots in Flintshire, being the daughter of Ann Jones whose parents were David Jones and Ann Williams of Tremeirchion. Ann Jones married Joseph, the son of Colonel Francis Scourfield who hailed from Pembrokeshire, and Jane Ann Scourfield subsequently married Robert Mills. To date it has proved impossible to flesh out a fuller account of Rhoscomyl's family history, other than to add that his mother re-married, moved to Manchester, and died on 5 March 1869, survived by Rhoscomyl and his sister, Ada, whose dates of birth and death are at present not known, and whose course in life remains uncharted.[4]

What befell Rhoscomyl between the age of six and sixteen appears to have revolved around his maternal grandmother, the remarkable Ann Scourfield (née Jones), who is thought to have brought him up in Tremeirchion where, David Littler Jones assures us, no one had ever heard of him when he tried to pick up his trail in 1991. He drew a blank, as did the reporter for *The Rhyl Advertiser* in 1919 when he sought information about Rhoscomyl's childhood. Similarly, there is no mention of Ada. Local historians have struggled to unearth factual information about Ann, but her date of birth is given as 5 November 1797 and she is said to have died in 1879 following an eventful life, including three marriages, the second of which, to a Mormon whose surname was Gill, took her on her travels as far as Salt Lake City. Indeed, she is reputed to have visited North America twice before 1840, and when Rhoscomyl undertook a journey through thirteen states at the beginning of the 1880s, one of his letters tells how he got to a place near Illinois 'where Granny lived and I stayed with people that knew and respected her'. Reputed to have been a beautiful woman, a good dancer, and to her family 'an ancestor . . . more fun than all the rest put together', she cries out for reincarnation in a novel.[5]

That his 'Granny' exerted a lasting influence on Rhoscomyl is certain. His lifelong intrepidity bore her stamp, but by far the most dominant aspect of her hold on him is to be traced to the fervour with which she regaled her young grandson with tales of the heroes of Welsh history. That he was later in life to adopt Arthur Owen Vaughan as his preferred name is directly attributable to her enthusiasm for King Arthur, and more especially, Owain Glyndŵr, whose patronymic was Fychan (Vaughan). Adamant that she could trace her descent back to Dafydd, the butchered brother of the butchered Llywelyn, the Last Prince of Wales (Llywelyn Ein Llyw Olaf), she captured Rhoscomyl's imagination, convincing him of a former glory long lost, but not beyond recovery, and in her championing of Owain Glyndŵr made Rhoscomyl for ever his liegeman.

Ann Scourfield was the Sybil who early on prepared Rhoscomyl for his forays into the past of Wales, and her presence is tangible in his *Flame-Bearers of Welsh History*, commissioned and published in 1905 by the Welsh Educational Publishing Company for the benefit of the nation's schoolchildren. In 1945, as Hitler's tyranny collapsed, it was the discovery of this book in the pitch-pine bookcase in our primary school at Llanddewi Aber-arth, and in particular the coloured depiction of the isolated Llywelyn's pitiless death, that first stirred in me a realization that we, the Welsh, had long, long ago been at the receiving end of tyranny's lances. Despite a literary style that I found somewhat forbidding, I read the book through, and still recall my

DEATH OF LLYWELYN

sense of elation on finishing it. It has now occupied an honourable place on my bookshelves for longer than I care to remember.

What happened to Rhoscomyl between his grandmother's death and his participation in the Boer War is fertile territory for fiction. Various accounts tell how he left Porthmadog as a stowaway on a brig bound for Rio de Janeiro (Amlwch is also named as his point of departure in his papers), and how, on making land, his life subsequently erupted in a succession of escapades often bordering on the fantastic. The introduction to his 'Western', *Lone Tree Lode* (1913), tells how the hero, David (Dai) Jeffreys, on his fourteenth birthday, left his home, an old farmhouse 'under the shoulder of the vast Pumlimon mountain', to go to sea with one of his father's cousins, sailing out of Aberdovey with slates for Galveston, Texas: 'At Galveston the lure of the Wild West had been too strong for him, and he had bolted from the ship.' Lest his mother should worry herself to death he sent her letters, in Welsh, telling of his whereabouts and activities, out of which he then fashioned *Lone Tree Lode*. This 'explanation' endorses a similar introductory explanation to *A Scout's Story* (1908), something of a killing spree with a cinematic potential worthy of Sam Peckinpah's invention, and it would appear fairly safe to assume that Rhoscomyl's youthful passage to South America is indeed more fact than fiction.[6]

The exuberant opening sentence of the first letter in *Lone Tree Lode* brings into view an unfettered cowpuncher: 'I left El Paso, on the Rio Grande, on the day I was sixteen, having made up my mind to go and see the great new ranges they are opening up in Wyoming, at the end of the Northern Trail, where the buffalo are being cleared out to make room for cattle.' A series of thirteen letters written between May 1880 and November 1884 follows the progress of a soon-to-be hard-bitten cowboy as he traverses the ranges from Colorado, through Wyoming to California, learning the rules by which the cowboys lived: 'In this country it is everybody's business to look after himself and to keep himself alive the best way he knows how'; 'Nobody ought to come to the West unless they can take their medicine when it comes as it comes, whatever it is, and keep a stiff upper lip about it too' (this after describing a lynching); and 'the one supreme crime for which the West has no forgiveness' – the desertion of one's 'pard'.[7]

But there was considerably more than cowpunching to Rhoscomyl's life in North and South America. *A Scout's Story* and *Lone Tree Lode* are about the hunt for gold, and there were always Indians and buffaloes to fight and butcher. In 1909 Sir Marchant Williams, loud in his praise of him in *The Nationalist*, summarized Rhoscomyl's exploits in a passage which *The Western Mail* lifted for its obituary in 1919:

> So young was he in years and appearance that when camping out with the gypsies of the West, when tracking Indians and hunting buffaloes, when in prison with the rest of a mutinous crew in the Western Islands, and when doing dazzling deeds of daring and valour in the Rockies or at the foot of the Andes, he was always treated fondly by his wild companions and always known as 'The Kid'. Sometimes a sympathetic British Consul would put him on a ship bound for this country, but it was always for no purpose, for his home was on the high seas and in the wild places of the earth.[8]

'THE KID'

Rhoscomyl, it appears, had even tried his hand at piracy and he would give rein to his enthusiasm for the daring of the Welsh breed of pirate in another of his romantic novels, *The Jewel of Ynys Galon* (1895).

A letter written in something of a breathless rush in 1943 by his niece, Dorothy Stott, has Rhoscomyl after his return from the West, and a brief enlistment in the army, on a kind of tireless, battle-hungry charge in various countries. We are told that he returned, aged twenty-one (in 1884), to stay with his sister Ada for a while and that he joined the army after failing to join the expedition that went in search of Livingstone. (He would have been eight years of age in 1871!) She obviously had in mind H.M. Stanley's 1884-7 expedition to the Congo. On leaving the army, so Dorothy Stott tells us, he took to writing fiction, but there was no domiciliating the action man:

> From this time all his life was spent as a mixture of fighting and writing. He had his own men who fought under him and he helped several other countries, for example he was sent for to take the King and Queen of Servia to safety but arrived too late. He helped the young King of Portugal after the massacre of the King and Crown Prince. Then he fought for America in Cuba, from there he went to South Africa taking with him some of his men who fought with him as scouts all through the Boer War. There he took one name after another as the enemy learnt his identity.[9]

America's war against Spain in Cuba in 1898-9 is a known fact, as is the assassination of King Alexander of Serbia in his Belgrade palace in 1903, and likewise the assassination of King Carlos I of Portugal together with the heir to the throne, in 1908. As for Rhoscomyl's actual involvement in these events there is nothing to add in the absence of corroborative detail, and Dorothy Stott's allusions merely highlight Rhoscomyl's ripeness for fictional treatment. With Bryn Owen, the author of *Owen Rhoscomyl and the Welsh Horse* (1990), we are on firmer ground. He gives 1887 as the year of Rhoscomyl's return to Britain, having as believed served since 1885 as a volunteer with the Canadian Militia 'during the suppression of Riel's Second Revolt against the Canadian Government'. According to Bryn Owen it was a desire to join Stanley's Congo venture, 1884-7, that prompted his return, and on failing he then joined the 1st Royal Dragoons as a private, hoping to see action in Egypt and the Sudan. But Rhoscomyl, finding regular soldiering much too uneventful for his liking, obtained his discharge from the army in 1890 and took to writing historical romances before returning to America, at some unknown date, to fight against the Spanish forces in Cuba as one of Theodore Roosevelt's 'Rough Riders' The outbreak of the Boer War in 1899 brought him galloping back to join the fray in South Africa and from then until his death in 1919 we have a clearer picture of his activities.[10]

Rhoscomyl's foray into the West is fated to remain a fragmented story but one thing is certain – 'The Kid' who survived the exhausting hazards of climate and wilderness while contending with the rage of displaced natives and the villainy of various desperadoes emerged as a formidable fighting horseman who, it appears from his writings, had a killer instinct in battle allied with an unnatural, if not pathological, disregard for danger and personal preservation. What is more, judged on the evidence of *A Scout's Story* and *Lone Tree Lode*, which parade a lethal prejudice against the native Indians of North and South America bearing the trademark of Victorian bloodsoaked racism, Rhoscomyl returned from the American continent a confirmed imperialist such as Roosevelt, who advocated 'smashing the tribal mass', would have welcomed. Neither novel is a conventional cowboy story. They are essentially imperialistic quests for gold and in the telling they take for granted the right of the civilized white hunters to 'wipe out' all native opposition to their plundering. Rhoscomyl's gold-seekers, with the Welsh to the fore, are indeed worthy descendants of 'stout Cortez'.

In *A Scout's Story*, Caradoc leads his Christian gold-craving, land-grabbing, revengeful band in pursuit of giant, sun-worshipping Indians who have taken the blue-eyed, blonde, hymn-singing Dilys captive, to be sacrificed to their gods as punishment for the theft of their gold. The mere thought of her rape by savages – rape in all its manifestations

DILYS PRAYS FOR DELIVERANCE

being the white man's prerogative – turns Caradoc into a killing machine. These pagan 'others' must be slaughtered for civilization to advance. Dilys is rescued, Welsh resolve and progressivism – they even manage to build a steamboat in the wilderness – triumph over all obstacles, culminating in the total defeat of a spear-carrying enemy, thousands strong, by a force of eighty mounted warriors armed with rifles which they fire with unerring imperialistic aim. The fact that the Indians had been robbed in the first place does not give pause to the settlers intent on revenge and loot. Qualms of conscience can be laughed away. As Coos, their Boer ally, tells Ephraim:

You ought not to feel squeamish. Do as you all did when you marched up to steal a couple of countries and all the gold and diamonds and people in them. Just say, 'Transvaal!' and ride in.

To which Ephraim replies:

Yes . . . Let's do as the Boers did when they first went to the Transvaal – proclaim ourselves a Republic, elect ourselves into the Government of it, and proceed to take possession of the resources of the country – and everything else we take a fancy to. How'll that do?

Whereupon Coos 'roared out with a great laugh, and we all joined in'.[11]

Justice, let alone mercy, is not for the 'lesser breeds'. At the end of *A Scout's Story*, the temple of gold is set alight and the molten metal runs down into the fathomless lake below. Imperialism, however, will return with technology in its train – and it will prevail:

But we are preparing another expedition for next summer, with machine guns and plenty of ammunition, and such things. We shall also take with us steam windlasses and thousands of fathoms of wire rope and grappling-hooks, to grapple for gold. We shall do everything scientifically, and, if there is no other way, then we shall tunnel the ridge and drain the lake off into the Pagans' Valley, getting at the gold that way.

THE LURE OF GOLD

There's such millions of it. It would be a sin to let all that gold lie wasted. [12]

Again, in *Lone Tree Lode*, the extermination of unassimilable native Indians who come between the expropriating whites and their gold proceeds with Darwinian inevitability. The location of the wondrous lode is known to the old, cultured, university-educated 'Captain'. He will show the way and Young Tex, a Welshman, together with his partners, will kill with bullets and dynamite anything, and if necessary everything, that stands in their way. After a skirmish in which some renegade Indians are killed, Young Tex finds one who is not yet dead of his wounds and they 'finish him off':

> When we came to the wounded Indian, sitting hunched up on the prairie, two or three of the men pulled out their six-shooters just as they would have done to a wounded wolf. The Indian saw it and tried to stand up, but failed till the first shot struck him. That spurred him and he rose straight up to his feet, struck out his chest, and waited for the rest as proud as steel. 'That's fine! That's good! Heap big Injun!' cried the men, as they fired again till they dropped him.
>
> I think the Indian heard them quite clearly, and was proud of it as his life went out.[13]

Their demonstration of racial superiority summarily concluded, they then lynched Black Hank with similarly expeditious righteousness.

There are no reviews of any substance to tell us how a Welsh readership responded to Rhoscomyl's stories of brutal imperialism at work. Two of his historical romances, *Battlement and Tower* and *For the White Rose of Arno* received brief notice in *The Times*[14] as 'boys' stuff', and when Roland Mathias published his *Anglo-Welsh Literature: An Illustrated History* in 1986, he had little more to add:

> If most of his books can be catalogued as 'For boys, young and old', they are nevertheless a Welsh contribution to the honourable school of Ballantyne and Henty, and the impossibility in the later twentieth century of reproducing their attitudes in new writing should be enough to secure their historical value for modern readers.[15]

Fair comment for sure.

When Beriah Gwynfe Evans, a would-be novelist and dramatist better fitted for pageantry, wrote about 'Wales in Fiction' for *Wales: To-day and To-morrow* (1907), he was mainly concerned to dismiss Allen Raine – highly regarded by Rhoscomyl – as a convincing portrayer of Welsh 'gwerin' life. For Evans she was Rhoscomyl's inferior despite the fact that he had only achieved a 'qualified success' in his historical romances, not having 'attempted to picture for us the Welsh peasant in such a little gem as that in which he presents American cowboy life in his inimitable *The Kid*'. Unlike Raine, Rhoscomyl knew his limitations. The problem he posed the reader was 'whether to label an historical work as a romance, or one of his novels as history'.[16]

O.M. Edwards certainly shared Rhoscomyl's appreciation of Raine's novels, but what he thought of stories such as *Old Fireproof*, *A Scout's Story* and *Lone Tree Lode* he appears to have kept to himself. As a matter of policy he seldom reviewed novels in *Cymru*, but it would be interesting to know if his lifelong love for the Welsh 'gwerinwyr' (folk) had room also for those 'cheap races' Rhoscomyl's riders seemed always primed to kill. Would the Calvinistic imperialist in him that with a zeal fit for a Kipling sent his son, Ifan, to fight the Hun in the Great War have found them as alienating as Jews and Catholics? If only we knew what he and Rhoscomyl talked about. Given the Welsh response to both the Boer War and the Great War it seems safe to assume that in Liberal, chapel-going Wales, Rhoscomyl would have found readers eager for the kind of story he had to tell about their boys' exploits in the killing fields of empire. The Welsh were up for it.

It was his belief that Wales had never been recognized, let alone rewarded, for its fighting contribution to the creation of the incomparable British Empire that determined Rhoscomyl's slant on Welsh history. His conduct throughout the Boer War was that of a battling 'Cymro' who had taken upon himself at the zenith of imperial power the vindication of 'an old and haughty nation, proud in arms'. Lieutenant Colonel Sir Reginald Rankin, who wrote *A Subaltern's Letters to his Wife* (1901), tells how Rhoscomyl, who served at one time as a sergeant in his troop, had rushed out to South Africa immediately on returning to England 'from the ends of the earth'. On getting to Southampton and finding the vessel full and about to sail, he duped a drunken second-class passenger by plying him with more drink, taking his ticket from his pocket, and departing with his luggage at the last moment: 'Not requiring two lots of luggage, he gave the second-class passenger's effects to the steward, and was subsequently very well waited on all the way to Capetown.'[17]

It is little wonder that O.M. Edwards had his work cut out as mediator when Rhoscomyl, who would certainly have expected praise for his resourcefulness, thought himself characterized as a common thief by Rankin, one of Edwards's old students at Oxford. It did not help that Rankin had introduced him in his book as 'a sergeant with about fourteen initials in front of an assumed name, who admitted that he was better than he appeared to be, and no better than he should be, for which latter reason he found it convenient occasionally to vary his signature'. It was hardly a testimonial for a former cowboy whose boast was that his character had been fashioned by the black-and-white morality of the Wild West.

But notwithstanding Rhoscomyl's resentment of what he thought were slighting personal remarks, there was no mistaking Rankin's admiration for the fighting 'olive-skinned, black-moustached dare-devil with the round head and piercing eye of the true Celt' who told him 'that he spent his life hurrying from one fight to another, and when there was no fighting worth the name going on in a pacific world . . . was in the habit of taking a little house in Wales, wherein the reading of Welsh history and the drinking of sparkling Burgundy constituted his favourite pastimes'. That 'wonderful man', said Rankin, 'was, after my dear friend Hubert Howard, the bravest man I ever came across. He volunteered on every occasion for the most risky work, and he took a real pleasure in courting danger.' Such was his recklessness that there was talk in the regiment that he had come to South Africa to put an end to an unhappy life, but Rankin thought for that theory to be true 'he must have developed unhappiness at a very early age; for on his own confession he had fought in nearly every campaign of the last twenty years'.[18]

Bryn Owen's sketch of Rhoscomyl's involvement in the Boer War leaves us in no doubt about his extraordinary aggression and decisiveness. His obituary in *The Western Mail* also tells how, as soon as he landed in Cape Town, he immediately set about raising a troop of Welsh Horse from among the refugees from the Transvaal and other South African colonies, gathering together two whole squadrons within the space of two days. When they were rejected he travelled 200 miles by train to De Aar, got up another local troop for defensive purposes, and on the arrival of regular cavalry took his men, 'men reckless and headlong, fearing neither God nor man, so common repute spoke of them', to join General Rimington's Guides. Serving as one of some eighty scouts for those Guides, approximately 180 strong, 'a hard riding crowd, well disciplined under the hand of their Colonel and drawn from a mixture of native Colonials, Britons and even a detachment of Argentinian Gauchos', Rhoscomyl put his experience in the Indian Wars to fierce use against the Boer's devastating guerrilla tactics. He was quickly promoted to sergeant, was mentioned in despatches and before the end of the war had been commissioned, going on to serve 'as a Squadron Commander with Damant's Horse and as Wing Leader of Canadian Scouts'.[19]

In 1902, the 'Honours and Awards List' published in the *Army and Navy Gazette* noted that Rhoscomyl had been awarded the Distinguished Conduct Medal. Despite the disappearance of the official Citation accompanying the award, Bryn Owen believes that the following story, published in the *Regimental Journal of The Welch Regiment* in the early 1930s, may well have been drawn from the actual Citation. It certainly bears the hallmark of Rhoscomyl's fearlessness:

> One day during the War, a British Patrol was retiring, hotly pursued by Boers, when a Trooper of the rearguard had his horse shot from under him just as he approached the banks of a river which his comrades had just crossed. Pinned down by his horse, and with the Boers close at hand, it looked as if his number was up. Vaughan [Rhoscomyl] was already across the river, but on seeing the plight of his comrade, turned and without hesitation recrossed the water to his assistance. Freeing the man, he lifted him across the front of his saddle, and under a hail of fire, brought him to safety.

What better illustration could there be of Rhoscomyl's enduring belief, as expressed in *Lone Tree Lode*, that there could be no worse betrayal than the desertion of one's 'pard'? His men, as described by the Brigadier-Major in *Old Fireproof*, were 'the riff-raff of the wide world . . . and of half its breeds, Greeks and Poles, Turks, and what not, even Jews; men that no one else will have, or could handle or do anything with if they had them . . .' But they were 'masters of battle work' and on that account they were in 'the Captain's' (Rhoscomyl's) eyes, 'marvels' not to be forsaken.[20]

A RIMINGTON SCOUT TO THE RESCUE

General Bruce Hamilton, Brigadier-General Rimington and Lieutenant General Hutton were to endorse Rankin's estimation of Rhoscomyl's exceptional valour. For Hamilton he was simply 'the bravest man I have ever met'. Rimington characterized him as 'a most dashing leader' who 'on innumerable occasions . . . showed the greatest skill and absolute disregard of danger. First in the attack and last to retreat, he made himself a name for daring wherever he went, and his example was of the greatest value.' Hutton averred that: 'There was no one . . . who did better or more gallant work as a scout and a leader of reconnoitring parties than Captain Vaughan when serving with my mounted force.' Such praise from his superiors was testament to a tremendous fighting spirit which was recognized in like measure by his fellow troopers. Known as the 'Tigers' (despite there being no tigers in South Africa), each member of Rimington's Guides wore a piece of leopard skin under his cap band, but the leopard's claw, the uncontested proof of a rare fighting man in their midst, was awarded to Rhoscomyl by Colonel Damant, Rimington's successor, since it was he, according to Damant, who always did the striking. The story gains in the telling when Damant is reported to have made his decision on seeing Rhoscomyl return to camp in the early morning 'with wounded and prisoners after a successful midnight raid'.[21]

As if harrying and killing the Boers was not action enough for him, in the course of the war Rhoscomyl took the outrageous step of marrying one of their daughters unbeknown to her family. Were it not that he brought his wife back to Wales with him and fathered four children in the course of a loving marriage, one might be tempted to think of him as a latter-day Bois Gilbert lustfully spiriting away another Rebecca. He was thirty-seven years of age and Catherine Lois de Geere (also written as Katherine Louisa) was eighteen. A letter among his papers in the National Library of Wales describes the wedding on the banks of the river Vaal, near Vredefort in the Northern Free State, witnessed by Mrs Dupree, Catherine's sister, and Sgt-Major Tom Harvey who had secured an English nonconformist minister (whose name has not survived) to conduct the ceremony 'as no Boer minister would marry us':

> There was shooting by the outposts while we were being married and bullets through the leaves overhead and about us. The minister wrote out a certificate which I kept, as my wife's people would destroy it if they found it on her. I had brought her out there because it would have been impossible to marry her in Vredefort unless we had been occupying that town. Moreover it had to be a secret for my wife's sake, as she would have to stay there in her mother's house, while I rode on with the column. I wanted to make sure she couldn't marry anyone else, so that I could get her again at the end of the war if we both survived. I think it was the 21/12/1900.

It was a wedding such as only Rhoscomyl could have desired – a lively skirmish with bullets for confetti.[22]

Sgt-Major Tom Harvey died of his wounds before the war ended and Mrs Dupree perished of a fever in Vredefort Road concentration camp. The anonymous minister who married Rhoscomyl and Catherine, having left South Africa to undertake missionary work, also died of a fever, and the marriage certificate was destroyed when a badly wounded Rhoscomyl was carted to a field hospital where he was stripped and his blood-soaked uniform burned. At the end of the war he had no way of proving that he was married to a Boer girl and no papers to secure their passage to Britain. Needless to say, he did bring her back with him, they did eventually, after brief sojourns in Fegla Fawr near Barmouth, and then in Cardiff, make their home in Dinas Powys and bring up four children, two boys and two girls, and when Catherine died aged forty-five in 1927, she was buried with her husband under the Celtic cross that marked his grave in the old cemetery in Rhyl.[23]

Even allowing for the wondrous ways of love, theirs could never have been an easy relationship. The Boer War was a pitiless affair that reduced the 'superior' kind of British Aryan imperialism to the foul expedient of erecting concentration camps in which thousands perished, including at least two members of Catherine's family (her sister, the aforementioned Mrs Dupree, and a nephew of hers also) and in one of

COLONEL RIMINGTON'S NOTORIOUS SCOUTS, 'THE TIGERS', FROM *THE BOER WAR* BY THOMAS PAKENHAM

(George Weidenfeld & Nicolson Ltd), reproduced with kind permission

THE BRAVEST OF THE BRAVE

which she, too, is said to have spent some time suffering from a bout of dysentery. The depth of residual bitterness would not soon be bridged, and life's hurts in a strange country, the antipathy of her husband's family in particular, were deepened for Catherine by a constant want of money and a distressing realization, as her daughter Olwen put it, 'that it was common report that she was a negro'. And Dinas Powys as representative of 'gallant little Wales' was sufficiently familiar with the racist scale of things in turn of the century Britain to know that the Celts, if not featuring highly in that scale, at least insisted on taking precedence over negroes. Olwen much regretted her mother's straitened circumstances when Rhoscomyl died, his estate valued for probate at a mere £85, leaving her without a pension (she had no marriage certificate to prove she was his rightful widow) and facing debts of £400 which necessitated selling Vron, their home, and all its contents excepting their personal belongings. Katherine Louisa Vaughan, the thirteenth child of a Boer farmer in the Orange Free State and a bright young girl who had studied mathematics in a Cape Town college, certainly did not marry for money and easy living when she gave her hand to Rhoscomyl.[24]

What, then, triggered such an unlikely romance? Marrying Rhoscomyl, of course, could deliver Catherine from a fate similar to that of her sister, but her Boer fortitude precludes such an explanation. It has to be sexual attraction. Catherine was loth to talk, even to Olwen, about her love-life, not wanting it cheapened by 'this age of advertisement at all cost'; she was, however, keen to impress upon her 'that I never captured him nor forced him to marry me at the point of a pistol!' But shortly before her death in 1927 she wrote these revealing words:

Now the true romance between your daddy and me lay in the fact that my voice when I first spoke to him ran like music (according to him) and I was good to behold, and it was love at first sight with him. And he was 37 and a hardened lover. With me it was otherwise. I thought him ugly, insignificant, and not the kind of knight in armour whom I had pictured in my day

CATHERINE LOIS DE GEERE
(By permission of the National Library of Wales)

dreams. Girls in those days did not dream about capturing the world. Only one man in it. And he being a Welshman, very artfully and skilfully made me see him as that knight of my dreams! And to me he is still the one man.[25]

Rhoscomyl 'the hardened lover'! Catherine Lois de Geere must have been some woman.

Olwen was told to read *Old Fireproof* if she wanted to learn more about her parents' falling in love and there is no missing the frisson of sexual excitement in the description of their first encounter in that thinly veiled fictionalized account of Rhoscomyl's exploits in the Boer War. In his story, narrated by the chaplain, Mr Allen, 'the Captain' (Old Fireproof) emerges as a life force, his lethal effectiveness in battle balanced by a sedulously acquired scholarly wisdom and a sound, no-nonsense Christian application of principles which mark him as a man apart. It goes without saying, of course, that he is at all times a staunch Welsh patriot. Catherine, for her part, comes into his life when, searching for information at the dead of night in a Boer 'dorp' he enters the wrong house and she confronts him. As a Boer commando she is later captured and sentenced to imprisonment in 'the Cage', only to be delivered by 'Old Fireproof''s insisting on them marrying, which she is powerless to resist. The chaplain marries them in the General's quarters in a ceremony that mirrors the one actually conducted on the banks of the Vaal, and then, by sheer force of will (strictly a thing of the spirit not of the flesh) 'Old Fireproof' forces her to admit that she loves him, and from then on their union is truly sanctioned.

It is Lieutenant Mansel, 'Old Fireproof''s 'pard' on the search for information, who describes Catherine's beauty to the chaplain as he tells of her sleepy emergence, lamp in hand, from the darkness, but it is Rhoscomyl, his imagination alight with the depiction of Olwen in the native Welsh romance, *Culhwch ac Olwen*, and his ardour aflame with the memory of his actual meeting with Catherine, who brings her desirability pulsing into life:

Tall she was, and shaped as the hand of God Himself would shape a girl in her glory. White she was, all white and white again, from the white of her round smooth neck to the white of her foot, where the hem of the fringing lace half hid her instep. Dark her hair was, dark and soft as the clouds that pass at dawn, a wide floating mass that was kept from her eyes by a broad black band of velvet round her forehead, and then went spreading softly down to below her waist. And except for the dark of her hair, and the blackness of that velvet band, there was no spot of colour in all the picture of her, except one great pink rose pinned between her breasts; a rose that had been crushed a little – showing that she had lain uneasily, unable to sleep – but still a rose and sweet to see, and right to see, there on her breast.[26]

Here is the love of Rhoscomyl's life and one would have thought her beauty needed no extolling at the expense of others, but even in love he could not withstand the urge to vanquish. A fully-fledged reactionary on the question of women's rights, he followed his shaft of love with a bolt of spleen directed at the suffragette:

Man! What a thing it is to see a woman that God made and that towns have never spoilt: a sweet, soft, proud girl like that, that all men have to bend their necks to. So splendid! – and then think of the squealers about women's rights! Did you ever see one of those squealers that were anyway balm to a man's eyes to see them?[27]

Olwen, his daughter, recalled a loving, dutiful father, but he was a man who knew, and expected the woman to know, her proper place. The theatre of war was certainly no place for her – what, one wonders, would he have had to say to Vera Brittain, author of the memorable *Testament of Youth* – and Catherine, whether willingly or not, appears to have concurred with his views. In her own words:

Perhaps he felt the underlying sense of self-advertisement that activated so many females. I may be wrong and he may be wrong. He fitted in more with Drake's time, according to Lord Howard [de Walden]. And I was weaned on Scott and [Bulwer] Lytton.[28]

The more one thinks of Catherine, the more one marvels at the resolve that led her to marry the tirelessly combative Rhoscomyl and leave her country to live with him, most of the time in poverty, among strangers. Resolute of heart and steadfast in her love, life could indeed have dealt her a more rewarding hand.

For Rhoscomyl there was to be one more war to fight. He was fifty-one years of age when the Great War broke out in 1914 and he would serve to its calamitous end in 1918. In *The Western Mail* he urged his countrymen to arm themselves with all speed to ensure the total defeat of the enemy, while he wasted no time in setting about recruiting a force of Welsh Horse and 'persuading' Kitchener to recognize them. Bryn Owen's clear account of Rhoscomyl's ambition to establish a Welsh Regiment of Horse Guards – St David's Horse – for service with the Household Brigade, of his success in forming a mainly Glamorgan-sponsored regiment of over 2,000 horsemen to fight the Kaiser, and of his intense disappointment on seeing the command denied him in favour of Hugh Edwards, 6th Lord Kensington of Little Haven, Pembrokeshire, obviates any need to pursue the story further. Suffice it to say that Rhoscomyl's abrasive manner and uncompromising Welshness led to him falling foul of the Glamorgan Territorial Force Association presided over by the Earl of Plymouth, and as the War Office had finally decided, much to Rhoscomyl's dismay, to accept the Welsh Horse as a Territorial Force Yeomanry Regiment, that Association would determine its command. It was the Brigade-Major who said of 'the Captain' in *Old Fireproof*: 'If he could throttle that temper of his, he'd be a general before the war's out.' Rhoscomyl did not even make the short list. In his own words he 'was awarded the order of the boot. A real live lord got the regiment.' In 1915 he would confide in a letter to his friend, Professor J. Glyn Davies:

> I didn't get the Welsh Horse, Glyn, because I'm Owen Rhoscomyl, and the 'County Families' of Glamorgan were dead off letting the stubbornest Welsh Nationalist in the County command any Regiment raised there.[29]

Indeed, as Bryn Owen tells us, he took no position with the Welsh Horse regiment, but on 29 September 1914 'he was gazetted Temporary Major in the 14th (Service) Battalion, The Northumberland Fusiliers'. His obituary in *The Western Mail* has it that having quickly understood that the Great War would be no war for horsemen, he transferred to a corps 'that was in the thick of the fighting in the chief zone of hostilities'. His undiminished, fearless commitment with the Fusiliers, then with the King's Own Yorkshire Light Infantry, and before the war ended as Lieutenant-Colonel with some 60,000 men of the Labour Corps under his command in the Ypres salient, was to win him the DSO and the OBE (Military Division) in January and June 1919.[30]

He returned from the Western front ever the hero, ever the begetter of stories about himself. How he would buttonhole those in highest authority in the War Office and tell them where they were going wrong. How it was 'known' that Lloyd George depended upon him for accurate reports on the situation at the front, sending him incognito to find out what the Generals were up to. George V, that mighty terminator of game birds, remembering Rhoscomyl's crucial role in the Investiture of the Prince of Wales in Caernarvon Castle in 1911, greeted him enthusiastically when on a morale-boosting visit to the troops, and took no offence when Rhoscomyl contradicted the royal assertion that Scotland had sent most recruits per head of population to the war. That distinction was due Wales – naturally – and Rhoscomyl was to prove his point.[31]

It was a rare Welshman who died of a carcinoma of the liver in a nursing home at 49 Beaumont Street, London, on 15 October 1919.

One for whom '[a]ll the sports of London Welsh life were ringing up offering their blood' when it was thought a transfusion could help him. He was in many respects the creature of a plundering, imperialistic age with a belief, as repellent as it was firm, in the rightness of dealing death to 'lesser breeds' opposed to the spread of empire. And yet he fell in love with, and married, a Boer's daughter, fathered a loving family and threw himself, heart and soul, into the promotion of what was considered a lower-case Celtic nation to which, by birth, he half belonged. The circumspect O.M. Edwards, while remarking on his strangeness, commended his honourable, gentlemanly nature, the childlike kindliness that merged so easily with his lionhearted bravery, his unfailing loyalty and patriotism. The tetchy Professor J. Glyn Davies, whose admiration for Rhoscomyl knew no bounds, recalled seeing him for the first time in 1903 in the University College Library at Aberystwyth, and of knowing without introduction who he was: 'But there was no mistaking the easy and virile bearing: it was not everyday insular British.' On the contrary he was a 'Frontiersman . . . I could hardly have missed.' And a certain Alban Morris of Cardiff, who first befriended Rhoscomyl in 1905, mourned his passing in verse which, if more partisan than poetic, resounds with a true sense of loss:

> Those starlit nights on veldt and prairie's face
> Didst fill with visions for thy company;
> But now, thou bravest falcon of the race,
> Thy hood is off for all eternity . . .

> Each moving pageant of thy eager will
> Rings with the music of thy son'rous name,
> Which, soldierwise, wert able to fulfil
> In life and work, at one with Cymru's fame.

It was Edward James, *The Western Mail*'s London correspondent, who said that: 'No passing caused a greater wave of emotion. Wales felt she had lost a giant.' And it was a *South Wales Daily Post* editorial that, after describing how Rhoscomyl sought hazards and exploits in the Elizabethan spirit 'with something of the versatility of a Raleigh imposed upon a Fluellen', concluded that he would be viewed in times to come 'as the most remarkable of contemporary Welshmen'. That he registered on a legendary scale in the consciousness of immediate post-war Wales was certainly beyond doubt.[32]

The question arises as to when this restless, fighting paladin aspired to be a serious Welsh historian. At what stage in his life did the interest aroused in him in childhood by his maternal grandmother mature into a determination to study and write about Welsh history from a committed patriot's point of view? Historical romances such as *The Jewel of Ynys Galon* (1895) and *Battlement and Tower* (1896) prove that he was feeling his way well before the Boer War, and his portrayal of 'the Captain' in *Old Fireproof* (1906) and 'the Professor' in *Lone Tree Lode* (1913) show that he sought recognition as more than a fighting man – no matter how awe-inspiring. He wanted to match 'the Captain' as a thinker, as a force for good in life. And as 'the Professor' complemented the pugnacity of Young Tex with his scholarly reading – the 'Odes' of Horace, Sir Thomas More's *Utopia* and John Lyly's *Euphues* – so Rhoscomyl also wanted to impress as a meditative man with an urge to write books, more especially books about early Welsh history. He would find himself in a neglected vineyard, labouring for a kind of harvest that apparently appealed little to the palate of more fastidious historians in Wales.

Before outlining his individualistic approach to his chosen field of study, it is as well to emphasize that a general appreciation of Welsh history as an energizing force in the life of the nation was hardly visible for most of Rhoscomyl's lifetime. On 3 September 1884 *The South Wales Daily News* published an article on 'Welsh Bards and Minstrels in Bygone Days' which had first appeared in *The Liverpool Mercury*, heralding the National Eisteddfod to be held in the city's North Haymarket, 15-20 September. Its inaccuracies triggered an exchange of letters between the usual assortment of eisteddfodic 'ancients and moderns', but what most mattered was highlighted in a *South Wales Daily News* editorial on 5 September.

It pointed out that the source of the offending article, according to one knowledgeable critic, was to be found in Edward Jones's *The Musical and Poetical Relicks of the Welsh Bards* (1784), whose 'authority' on such matters had been acknowledged in the ninth edition of *The Encyclopaedia Britannica* The very thought of 'accumulations of rubbish which go far to damage the Welsh in the eyes of their neighbours' being presented as history for inclusion in prestigious English publications was intolerable. The only answer to those few deluded Welshmen (obviously Iolo Morganwg's devotees) who persisted in disseminating 'the most crude, absurd, and damaging stories and impostures in the form of history', was to have written 'a good history of Wales for the people – a people's edition of such a history as our best Welsh scholars will not be ashamed to acknowledge and recommend'.[33]

Bearing in mind how Rhoscomyl in *Flame-Bearers of Welsh History* would seek to captivate and teach schoolchildren, it is noteworthy that *The South Wales Daily News* editorial of 5 September 1884 called for 'some eminent Welsh scholar' or other to provide for them, since 'it is in our schools that most people learn their history, and form their impressions of men and nations'. The importance of such a provision could not be overstated:

> It may seem a very small thing to ask a great scholar to take in hand, but when it is remembered that it concerns the name and the fame of their own fatherland, we hope they will not think that we are too exacting. Even children are entitled to the very best and the most reliable books. There is no reason in the world why they should have their minds deluged with absurdities which will stick for ever to them.

Moreover, once written these 'reliable' books shouldn't be confined to Welsh schools only but should be available 'in all the public elementary schools throughout the three kingdoms'. Welsh history mattered to the whole of Britain.

It was good that Thomas Powel, Professor of Celtic at University College, Cardiff, was to read a paper on 'The Place of the Welsh Language in our National Education' at the forthcoming National Eisteddfod in Liverpool, but as *The South Wales Daily News* saw things, 'we should hail with still greater satisfaction a paper by one equally qualified to deal with the question of "The Place of Welsh History in our National Education".' There was abundant room for improvement: 'Once let facts displace fiction in our schools, and rubbish-mongers will scribble in vain.' No such paper was read at Liverpool in 1884, but before the National Eisteddfod was over Professor John Rhŷs had awarded J.E. Lloyd, educated at Aberystwyth University College and Lincoln College, Oxford, a prize of £25 for an English-language text book on Welsh history for use in schools. What use was made of it and how influential did it prove to be are questions without answers, for it does not appear to have been published. The schools of Wales remained in the dark.

When (Sir) Isambard Owen (1850-1927) addressed the issue two years later before the Honourable Society of Cymmrodorion at the Caernarvon National Eisteddfod, he spoke not so much of a problem as of a crisis. A progressive educationist who was to leave his stamp on the Charter of the University of Wales and become its first Vice-Chancellor, his words carried weight when he said: 'The history of the Welsh people has become an almost forgotten study among its members. I do not know if in a single school in all Wales instruction in it is at this day given.' His view of things in 1886 was endorsed as late as 1912 by W. Llewelyn Williams, MP, who in the course of commending O.M. Edwards's part in arousing an interest in his country's past reminded his readers how very different things were twenty-five years before (circa 1887): 'Then no one made any pretence of knowing anything of Welsh history.'[34]

It is well to remember that Isambard Owen was talking at a time, and Llewelyn Williams of a time, when 'Cymru Fydd', the 'Young

Wales' movement, was creating something of a clamour for 'Home Rule' of sorts. It was bound to arouse dissent, and, as a perusal of *The Western Mail* in the 1880s shows, casting doubt on the genuineness of Welsh nationality proved yet again to be a popular oppositional ploy. At the beginning of February 1887, its druidically-inspired columnist, the unfettered Owen Morgan (Morien), addressing the question 'Is Wales a Nation?', tossed aside the contention of the *St James's Gazette* that it was 'absurd' to rate Wales as a separate nation, it being no more significant an entity than Kent or Northumberland. Morien, who had participated in the exchange of views in *The South Wales Daily News* in September 1884, insisted that: 'There never was a time in the history of Wales when its spirit of nationality was more keenly sensitive than it is at the present moment.' The Welsh had no wish to be seen as English surrogates: 'It is impossible to ignore at the present day the wonderfully renewed vitality of the Celtic races in these islands', a fact which served to reinforce the 'truth' that Wales had never been conquered and assimilated by England:

> The allegation that Wales was ever conquered is infamously untrue, as the best English historians candidly admit. England and Wales mutually agreed to the union of the two countries, and the union will ever continue to respect the proud national spirit of the Welsh people.[35]

It would be interesting to know what Edward I and Henry VIII would have made of Morien's tailored view of the past, but in fairness to him he was only practising the survivalist art of 'denial' without which Wales would have long been a mere acorn in the sow's belly of England.

But much more significant than Morien's not unexpected trumpeting of Welsh nationality was Gladstone's reaffirmation of it in Swansea on 4 June 1887, when some 30,000 supporters of the Liberal Federation heard him speak very clearly on the matter at Singleton Abbey. In the National Eisteddfod held in Mold in 1873, he had talked up the worthiness of Wales, to the great delight of his audience. Why, he asked again in 1887, if Welsh nationality was a mere chimera, had it been necessary in the past for its oppressors to build so many castles?:

> I affirm that Welsh nationality is as great a reality as English nationality (cheers). It does not extend over so great a part of the country, but in the traditions of Wales, in the history of Wales, in the language and religion of Wales, in the feelings of Wales, and in the intentions and determination of Wales, the Welsh nationality is as true as is the nationality of Scotland (to which by blood I exclusively belong) – as is the nationality of England (loud cheers).[36]

As Gladstone was at pains to emphasize, he was most certainly not encouraging disunion. On the contrary, he saw union threatened by anglocentric prejudices calculated to erode other nationalities and reduce them to pale imitations of the presiding central power. That way lay disaster: 'It is the mode at once to destroy strength and to mar and to break up union.'

'Cymru Fydd' would engender much rhetoric between 1886 and its demise in a sludge of anti-Welshness and rank chicanery at a 'fixed' meeting of the Liberal Federations of north and south Wales held in Newport in January 1896. Questions such as 'Was Wales ever a nation?', 'What is Welsh Patriotism?', 'Are the Welsh a nation?' would continue to exercise *The Western Mail*, which in 1889 seized upon Professor Boyd Dawkins's pamphlet, *The Place of the Welsh in the History of Britain*, as further proof that there were no grounds for believing 'that the Welsh are an unmixed race of people, constituted after a fashion which calls for a system of government altogether separate and distinct from that which is applied to their neighbours'. As compensation for patriots *The Western Mail* noted that Dawkins, in maintaining that both the Welsh and the English were 'mixed races', was more or less saying 'that the Welsh or Celtic strain has been crossed with the English or Teutonic, pretty nearly as largely as the latter has been crossed with the Celtic'. And that way lay salvation:

Our author pays the Welsh the high compliment of stating that 'some of them are descended from those who in remote ages introduced the first rudiments of civilisation, not merely into these islands, but into the whole of Europe, from the Rhine to the Straits of Gibraltar, and from the Alps to the shores of the Atlantic'. A people with a tradition like that has every reason to be proud.[37]

That *The Western Mail* in 1889 should see proof of Teutonic convergence as something to be prized above the realization of 'Cymru Fydd' aspirations is not surprising. The Teutons had long been thought to tower above the Celts as superior beings. Their history was of universal significance but what, if anything, was Welsh history about? The Bishop of St Davids, Dr William Basil Jones (1822-97), addressing the clergy of the Archdeaconry of Carmarthen at St Peter's Church, 28 September 1886, set about demolishing the case for disestablishment by denying the Welsh the right to be considered a separate nation meriting separate legislation to confirm its national identity and culture. He was comprehensively dismissive of Welsh particularities: 'Has Wales a common history? Has it a common centre of national life? If so, where is it? I answer, if anywhere, in London.' And, not leaving anything to chance, he added for good measure: 'In fact, Wales is at present nothing more than the highlands of England, without a "highland line". It is a geographical expression, nothing more.' Rhoscomyl would simply be entering another field of conflict in advancing his 'truth' about the history of Wales and the integrity of the national character.[38]

Writing in *The Welsh Leader* in 1905, the Reverend A.W. Wade-Evans, who was to make a sound contribution to Welsh historiography, could state that during sixteen years of education that took him from elementary school to Jesus College, Oxford, he was not taught a single lesson in the language, literature or history of Wales:

I lived over three years in a Grammar School which could in no way be distinguished from a similar institution in Norfolk or Kent, save that it was founded by a Welsh squire. And if it has been so with me who lived in the Welsh environment of North Pembrokeshire, what must it be with the Welshman of East Monmouth and Radnor? If it has been so with me who spoke Welsh as a child, what must it be with those who were brought up to regard Welsh as vulgar and the Welsh-speaking folk as deceitful? [39]

For Wade-Evans there could be no revival of national self-esteem without a restoration of Welsh history to a central place in national awareness. Welsh history was no mere 'miniature' of European history, a 'natural' understanding of which could only start for a child 'with his own patria – that is Wales, a patria which is by no means, as ignorantly supposed, a mere adjunct of England, but a separate cell in that multi-cellular unit as yet but indistinctly apprehended under such vague appellations as "Western Civilization".' And in a sentence that must have chimed perfectly with Rhoscomyl's beliefs in the year that saw *Flame-Bearers of Welsh History* published, Wade-Evans declared that:

> The realization of Welsh nationality in his own experience, is for the Welsh child the royal road to the realizing of the wider life of Europe, which again, in its turn, leads directly to a revelation of the human spirit, on a scale hitherto without precedent.[40]

In that same journal, that same year, the young J. Fred Rees, BA, (1883-1967), who was to distinguish himself as a Welsh historian and as the Principal of University College, Cardiff from 1929 to 1949, also protested against treating the history of Wales as merely 'a disturbing cause that forces the English central power to depart for a moment from its path of development'. The Welsh would become citizens of the world only by achieving a critical understanding of their own history, but for that to happen their national university would have to stop acting as if the old English canard, that the Welsh had no PROPER HISTORY, was an indisputable fact. It was in 1905, too, four years after publishing *Wales*, the first significant attempt at writing a popular history of the country in a single volume, that O.M. Edwards in *Cymru* repeated the accusation he had levelled against the University of Wales ten years earlier, in the periodical *Wales*, of discouraging the academic study of the language, literature and history of the nation it was meant to serve. His accusation was supported by the Reverend A. Wade-Evans who in August 1905 wrote bitingly about 'The Anglicizer' in *The Welsh Leader*.[41]

It was particularly galling for Victorian Wales, at a boom time in the writing of English history which served to underpin a widespread belief in England as 'the mighty necessity of civilisation', to find itself unable to turn its own history to good account after the 'Treachery of the Blue Books' in 1847 had inflamed a deep-rooted sense of inferiority and a concomitant fear of permanent inadequacy. The excoriation of a whole nation, as was thought, coincided with the publication in 1850 of *The Races of Man* by the Scotsman, Dr Robert Knox, which by promoting a hierarchical view of the human worth of different races and preaching that man was bound by his nature and his unchanging racial type, was to have a malign influence on the study of race relations down to the twentieth century.

Rhoscomyl was born into a race-soused century which by the 1860s had witnessed a splurge of vicious pseudo-sciences, such as racist-distorted human biology, ethnography, anthropology, phrenology and linguistics, all peddled in support of a polygenist challenge to the long-accepted monogenist position that imperial expansion, it was argued, had done so much to discredit. The disparity between the 'dear' and the 'cheap' races was so vast that the only sound explanation for it was that humankind had to be constituted of more than one species. Christianity's confirmation of the monogenist position should not be allowed to stand in the way of a 'scientific truth' that after 1859 could call on Darwinism, in some shape or form, to confirm *its* validity. Darwinism was Darwinism, no matter how coarsely applied.

Nancy Stepan in her authoritative study, *The Idea of Race in Science: Great Britain 1800-1960* (1982), has a splendid chapter on 'Race and the Return of the Great Chain of Being, 1800-1850', in which she shows how this medieval concept of a preordained order, in which every created thing was allocated its place according to its innate worth, re-surfaced to serve the arguments of Victorian racists. It became acceptable, even respectable, to determine the worth of different races and to grade them according to their perceived level of civilized development. There was no denying the hierarchy of human races, which invariably put the European at the top of the chain with the negro at the bottom. Science had merely to determine the best ways of measuring the obvious physical and cultural differences which denoted the inescapable reality of higher and lower orders.[42]

What is of particular interest in the context of Rhoscomyl's understanding of Welsh history is the way in which the Victorian grading of human races gave top billing to the Aryans, and none surpassed the English as the embodiment of those Aryan, in England's case, Teutonic powers, both intellectual and physical, that marked out a nation as predestined to conquer and rule over others. Celebrated as 'Anglo-Saxonism', simply the very essence of Teutonism, this supraexcellence which surged from within was, as Hugh A. MacDougal demonstrated in *Racial Myth in English History* (1982), to assume mythical proportions as some of the most influential historians of the Victorian age – Lord Macaulay, Thomas Carlyle, John Kemble, Goldwin Smith, J.R. Green, William Stubbs, J.A. Froude, Charles Kingsley, E.A. Freeman and Lord Acton – seconded in scholarly tones Martin Tupper's demotic adulation of 'The Anglo-Saxon Race':

> Stretch forth! Stretch forth! From the south to the north,
> From the east to the west, – stretch forth! stretch forth!
> Strengthen thy stakes and lengthen thy cords, –
> The world is a tent for the world's true lords!
> Break forth and spread over every place
> The world is a world for the Saxon race.

It would be for Lord Macaulay to say, in his own way, that the English were 'the greatest and most highly civilized people that ever the world saw'.[43]

Yes, scientific racism and a renewed belief in 'The Great Chain of Being' were to boost England's Teutonic Anglo-Saxon stock to very heady heights. 'Teutomania' would feature prominently in the English mindscape down to the outbreak of the First World War. But what of the Celts: how did they rate in the Victorian racist scheme of things? The answer, quite simply, is pretty low. They found themselves in the proximity of negroes ('nigger' became a term of racist abuse around 1857) and eskimos, branded a feckless lot given to bouts of 'wild hysterics' and damned for being by and large 'incapable of progress', at a time when a genius for PROGRESS was what put the English at the forefront of civilization.

In the 1860s a virulent 'Celtophobia', intensified by the Fenian bombing outrages in England, was given free rein in the press. 'Paddy' was lampooned as 'the missing link', his offensive prognathous jaw everywhere proof of a retarded state, and in Wales the newly-born National Eisteddfod, with foaming bards to the fore, was lined up by the London press for death by a thousand scornful cuts. It fell to *The Times* in September 1866 to voice the bitterest contempt for Wales, its language and culture, when the editor, Delaney, savagely rejected Matthew Arnold's contention that an England increasingly in the grip of a mercantile philistinism would greatly benefit from an infusion of Celtic spirituality and romanticism into its national being. The very thought that Wales could be to England what Greece had been to Rome elicited a response that remains a classic expression of 'Celtophobia':

> The Welsh language is the curse of Wales. Its prevalence and the ignorance of English have excluded, and even now exclude, the Welsh people from the civilization, the improvement, and the material prosperity of their English neighbours ... Their antiquated and semibarbarous language, in short, shrouds them in darkness ... If Wales and the Welsh are ever thoroughly to share in the material prosperity, and, in spite of Mr Arnold, we will add the culture and the morality of England, they must

forget their isolated language, and learn to speak English, and nothing else ... For all practical purposes Welsh is a dead language ... Wales, it should be remembered, is a small country, unfavourably situated for commercial purposes, with an indifferent soil, and inhabited by an unenterprising people ... A bare existence on the most primitive food of a mountainous race is all that the Welsh could enjoy if left to themselves ... All the progress and civilization of Wales has come from England, and a sensible Welshman would direct all his endeavours towards inducing his countrymen to appreciate their neighbours instead of themselves ... The sooner all Welsh specialities disappear from the face of the earth the better.[44]

It is as well to bear in mind that Rhoscomyl was born into a decade that quickened the pace of 'Celtophobia' and saw as a consequence an increased yearning among not a few Welsh people for the comfort of Aryan assimilation. The year of his birth, 1863, brought the National Eisteddfod to Swansea for the first time and Hussey Vivian, MP, used his presidential address to tell the Welsh how best to prepare for a profitable future:

At this time we are one whole united compact people. To the foreigners we are one ... Remember that you are all Englishmen though you are Welshmen ... Depend upon it we must consider ourselves Englishmen ... They in Wales ... thought England the greatest country in the world, and Wales the greatest country in England.[45]

He was supported by the first president of the National Eisteddfod Council, Rector John Griffiths of Neath, a 'Cardi' by birth and upbringing who, at a dinner celebrating the eisteddfodic union between north and south, made clear to whom they were truly indebted:

However infatuated Welshmen might be said to be, however hare-brained and enthusiastic, they were not such fools as to forget what Saxon intelligence, and Saxon energy, and Saxon money had done among them. Their advancement in national importance, in literature, in intelligence, in commerce, in everything good and great, was owing in a great measure to the energy and wealth of the Saxon.[46]

Little wonder that Rector Griffiths was much aggrieved by Delaney's assault three years later.

It was in that first Swansea 'National', too, that Dr Thomas Nicholas read his paper on 'High Schools and a University for Wales' at the behest of (Sir) Hugh Owen who had in 1862 grafted his 'Social Science Section' on to the eisteddfod tree. It was to lead to the opening of the first University College of Wales at Aberystwyth in 1872. Dr Nicholas was convinced that (I translate): 'perhaps the greatest blessing, next to Christianity, the gentle hand of Providence conferred on the Welsh, was the peace and social order resulting from their subjection under England's rule.' And any thought of them cultivating 'a narrow feeling of nationality' enraged him:

> Its root is ignorance, and its fruit disaster. Estrangement between two peoples under one rule helps only to starve the weaker . . . No valid reason exists . . . why the Welsh should not feel that they and the English are ethnologically one people, and it is better they should share in the honour and dignity, the intelligence and enterprise of England, than rest contented with the obscurity which blind adherence to antiquated customs, and to a speech which can never become the vehicle of science and commerce, must entail upon them. The Welsh, like the Scotch, should aspire to be in intelligence, enterprise, culture, all that the English are, feeling that, 'Frei athmen ist das Leben nicht.'[47]

When considering the role played by the University of Wales in the life of the nation, it helps to remember what a 'repellent' view of Welshness, as described by Professor Ieuan Gwynedd Jones, some of its prime promoters had at its inception and, I may add, how long such a view persisted, albeit in a less strident mode. Hugh Owen is ill served by latter-day apologists who seek to excuse his positivist unconcern for the fate of the Welsh language within his much longed for 'educational edifice'. He was no pussyfooter; English, for him, was the language of national salvation and, for him speaking as a confirmed technocrat, Welsh could quite simply go hang.

The point is made. Rhoscomyl grew up to hear too many of his compatriots singing 'I want to be like you' as they contemplated English supremacy. The evidence is overwhelming. John Eiddon Jones, writing in *Cymru Fydd* in April 1888, insisted that twenty or thirty years previously the Welsh feared extinction (*'difodiant'*). They didn't want to *think* about it, but (I translate): 'as far as we could see nothing else confronted us in the near future'. Even when celebrating St David's Day it was not unusual during the 1870s to hear the praises of England and the English sung loudest. In 1879, the year Rhoscomyl is said to have stowed away for Rio de Janeiro, St David was treated in Corwen to 'Rule Britannia' and 'What an Englishman is made of'. At the Talbot Hotel in Aberystwyth it was 'The Island home of an Englishman', 'A fine old English gentleman' and 'The Union Jack of Old England'. In Merthyr Tydfil, at the Castle Hotel, Mr T. Edwards in proposing a toast to 'Old England – including Wales' also gloried in the conquest that had tied the Welsh to a nation 'whose influence, language, and manners were fast becoming universal'. The way forward was clear:

> He was glad, as it were, to sink his own nationality, and it should be their duty to disarm their countrymen of the prejudices which so greatly kept the Welsh people back. They should go out into the world, become more cosmopolitan, and identify themselves more with England in all things, and then they would go on better than they had done.

From north to south the Welsh paddled happily in a tide of Anglophilia.[48]

As for Delaney's diatribe, it had to be condemned, as the three Commissioners' traducing of Wales in the Blue Books of 1847 had to be condemned, but that in no sense stilled a fear that what was broadcast with such vulgar certainty was cause for serious concern. If, as was said, the bedrock of sympathy between a leading and a led nation could only be 'like-mindedness' – which was Delaney's position – an etiolated Welshness had obvious benefits, and an accelerating disregard for the Welsh language to the point of total rejection was soon the order of the day for increasing numbers of Welsh people. Trumpeted as proof of a determination to PROGRESS, this spurning of the mother tongue was in fact mere cultural abasement, a psychological sickness which throughout the second half of the nineteenth century and forward into the twentieth had a thousand and one letter-writers flushing the pans of their self-disgust in our national press. (And they are still at it in the letters column of *The Western Mail*, our 'national' daily!) If, as Delaney thundered, one language sufficed for the English 'mass', why should the Welsh, of all people, aspire to speak two? Bilingualism hardly became so nondescript a people. The Welsh proceeded to build a system of education on the adoption of a Delaney-like Anglomaniac view of the rightness of things, and today a people for whom trilingualism, at least, should have been a valid educational aspiration, securing for Wales an enriching European presence, pays the price of its self-deprecation. In 2009, the material benefits confidently predicted in Rhoscomyl's day to accrue in a Welsh-free Wales do not loom large, but the cultural deficits are all too visible.

On his return to Wales from his wanderings, and as he began to contemplate life in Wales as a historian, Rhoscomyl would have quickly realized how conflicted the Welsh condition had been long before the Victorian age brought its own great pressures to bear on it. And he would not have had to search far and wide to find English historians ready to flaunt a sense of racial superiority at Wales's expense. In B.B. Woodward, E.A. Freeman and J.A. Froude he would have found three noteworthy contemporary examples of the breed.

Published in 1853, *The History of Wales from the Earliest Times* by B.B. Woodward, BA, who thought his ignorance of the Welsh language 'of comparatively little moment', had nothing less in mind than the deliverance of a people from a long-depressed state. Wielding the scalpel of 'living English', Woodward's aim was to cut out deep-rooted ills, especially 'the intense nationality of the Welsh' that 'makes historic impartiality impossible'. A ridiculous '"Pride" of ancestry' fertilized by 'the splendid exaggerations' of their bards had distanced the Welsh from reality, 'and history, in consequence, has partaken of the vagueness and mutability of dream-land'. The Welsh should desist from harbouring ancient resentment, and 'no longer striving vainly against *their appointed lot* [my italics], they must admit that what God's high providence has done, points out for them a path of action, sure of leading to great and desirable ends'. In virtue of racial distinction the English were God's annointed, and if the professed Welsh flair for worship amounted to anything, they should not find it anything but uplifting to aspire to be like their neighbours.[49]

In 1876 E.A. Freeman, author of the six-volume *History of the Norman Conquest* (1867-76), was elected president of the Cambrian Archaeological Association at its annual convention held in Abergavenny, thus crowning a relationship stretching back over some twenty-seven years, four of them, 1855-9, spent living in Llanrhymney Hall near Cardiff. Freeman was an incorrigible Teutonic racist who, on a visit to the United States of America in 1881, was heard to say: 'This would be a grand land if only every Irishman would kill a negro and be hanged for it.' It says much about the 'Welsh condition' in 1876 that his acceptance of the presidency gave great satisfaction. Freeman, for his part, appeared to take it for granted that he, 'purely Mercian by birth, purely West-Saxon in feeling', should be received so warmly by the 'Brets', the descendants of those whose fall he described with such relish.[50]

As a reward for their reception of him, after insisting yet again that the Teutonic element had long ago dominated the population of Britain, the majority of the Britons having been slaughtered and their remnants driven into Wales, Freeman, though adamant that Englishmen were not Welshmen, was happy to concede that 'Englishmen and Welshmen are alike kinsfolk of the common Aryan stock . . .' But for the Welsh, there was still the Iberian difficulty to be resolved. The Iberians were in Britain before the Celts arrived. What if it should transpire 'that there may be among us a considerable portion of ourselves and of our neighbours who do not belong to the Aryan stock at all?' It was a disturbing question, 'startling alike to the Celt and the Teuton, to the Briton and the Englishman; but it must be looked in the face'. It was in seeking a properly researched answer to it that Welsh historians could contribute to European history – despite the possibility of suffering a self-inflicted wound in the process:

> It would be strange, *and not altogether pleasant* [my italics], if the Silures and their famous Caradoc can be shown to be not Britons, not Aryans at all, but remnants of an earlier people who had at most adopted the tongue of Celtic conquerors. But, strange and unpleasant as the question may be, it is one which has to be answered; it is, I venture to say, the most important question which at this moment concerns the student of Celtic history and Celtic language.[51]

Yes, there was need of a scholarly history of Wales to facilitate the writing of a comprehensive history of England by historians such as Freeman. By neglecting that task the Welsh were doing the story of Empire a disservice. But strictly in a Welsh context the Iberian difficulty, while unresolved, cast doubts on racial integrity, and in Caradoc's case called into question the Aryan credentials of a long-acclaimed 'imperishable' Celtic-Welsh hero. The nation could ill afford the demotion through mongrelization of a hero such as Caradoc, as Freeman knew full well. The historian, J.W. Burrow, also knew full well what Freeman was about: 'Celts, for all that they were Aryan brothers, were objects of an obsessive hostility, and contempt; some Aryans were more Aryan than others.'[52]

Long an admirer of the Celt-spurning Scot Thomas Carlyle, J.A. Froude in 1887 published the first volume of *The English in Ireland in the Eighteenth Century*. He could see no answer to the perverse, violent Irish other than an 'efficient military despotism', but the manageable Welsh were to be commended for recognizing their limitations and submitting to government 'by those who are nobler and wiser than themselves'. Froude was at pains to emphasize that racial and cultural distinctiveness could in no sense justify the right to independence. A people's independence depended solely 'on the power of resistance . . . the right of a people to self-government consists and can consist in nothing but their power to defend themselves'. Civilization was basically a matter of clout – and the lack of it. The Welsh, to their credit, had seen that it was so:

> When resistance became obviously hopeless, they loyally and wisely accepted their fate . . . Yet, being wisely handled, restrained only in essentials, and left to their own way in the ordinary current of their lives, they were contented to forget their animosities; they ceased to pine after political liberty which they were consciously unable to preserve; and finding themselves accepted on equal terms as joint inheritors of a magnificent empire, the iron chain became a golden ornament. Their sensibilities were humoured in the title of the heir of the crown. In bestowing a dynasty upon England they found a gratification for their honourable pride. If they have contributed less of a positive strength than the Scots to the British Empire, they have never been its shame or its weakness; and the retention of a few harmless peculiarities has not prevented them from being wholesome and worthy members of the United Commonwealth.[53]

That such a demeaning commendation penned by a highly-regarded English historian could be published in 1887, the year of Victoria's Golden Jubilee, without putting backs up in Wales, is yet further proof of the debilitating effect of the 'amenable subject, imperial asset' syndrome on the Welsh sense of national worth. In their mother tongue, the Welsh cherished 'glân' (clean, pure) and 'llonydd' (passive, docile) as adjectives most apt to describe their conduct as England's readiest junior partner, for which Froude substituted 'harmless', 'wholesome' and 'worthy'. It was a Teutonic endorsement of a people who had no intention of allowing their Celtic past to obstruct their much sought for British advance – nor embarrass their present for that matter.

By the time Rhoscomyl set about turning his interest in Welsh history to some kind of affirmative use, he could not have failed to realize that in the course of a century that saw hero-worship pervading the cultures of England, the United States of America, and the countries of Europe, Wales had signally failed to capitalize on the renown of such figures as Caradoc, King Arthur, Llywelyn and Glyndŵr. Not that the wish to summon up heroes did not exist in Wales – Dr Tedi Millward has shown how eisteddfod poets aspired to write epic poems and how would-be novelists wrote serialized historical romances for the Welsh press. A literature celebrating a nation of brave people ('cenedl o bobl ddewrion') was indeed striven for, but the retreat of the Welsh language in the face of the incursions of the 'imperial tongue' undermined confidence and precluded popular appeal.[54]

It is, however, arguable whether by the Victorian heyday the majority of the Welsh were well disposed to the idea of elevating Llywelyn and Glyndŵr as heroes who had fought for the independence of their country against their English oppressors. While 'Teutomania' reigned there was a need for prudence, especially as some English historians still saw fit to dismiss the two Welshmen as mere rebels, brigands and traitorous malcontents. John Francis, a prominent Welsh Mancunian, argued strongly in the Denbigh Eisteddfod of 1860 for the restoration of 'a more British tone to the British people' in view of 'the somewhat excessive bias towards the German element in the English character', and he also castigated the Welsh people for a shaming reluctance, in comparison with other nations, to erect monuments in honour of their former champions and defenders. Like Sir James MacKintosh, he could also say of Wales 'that she thanklessly consigns to oblivion heroes whom Greece and Rome would have been proud to crown with the garland of immortality'.[55]

But the Welsh would not be so easily persuaded. A proposal to erect a national monument in memory of Llywelyn, the Last Prince of Wales, comparable with those 'noble structures' that were to commemorate William Wallace in Stirling and Daniel O'Connell in Dublin, was mooted in the famous Llangollen Eisteddfod of 1858. A good fifty years later the 'movement' ended in abject failure, less than £200 having been subscribed. It was one thing from the 1860s onwards to enjoy Llywelyn and Glyndŵr as entertaining, tuneful characters in innocuous Victorian musicals; it was another thing altogether to elevate them as stalwart fighters for Welsh independence when the accepted wisdom for many Welshmen was that their conquerors, in reality, had been their true benefactors. Patriotism, like money, needed canny husbandry.[56]

In 1855, Wales's most prestigious periodical, *Y Traethodydd* (The Essayist), published an article by R.J. Derfel (1824-1905) entitled *'Cymru yn ei Chysylltiad ag Enwogion'* (Wales in relation to famous people).[57] Derfel, who had made his home in Manchester and could claim to know the English at first hand, was already fiercely involved in countering the assault on the Welsh national character published in 1847 in the aforementioned Commissioners' Reports on the state of education in Wales. It was his satirical play, *Brad y Llyfrau Gleision* (The Treachery of the Blue Books), that pinpointed Wales's outraged response, while his lengthy article in *Y Traethodydd* should be seen as a blueprint for the recovery of national esteem. He bewailed the prevailing diffidence and the consequent want of celebrated Welsh heroes to raise Wales from its position of total insignificance among the countries of the world. As he put it, *'Gosodir ni yn is na phawb'* (We are placed lower than everyone). Should the Welsh nation disappear, the world would hardly notice the loss: *'Mae ein lle mewn hanesyddiaeth wedi cael ei ddwyn oddiarnom. Edrychir arnom fel cenedl wedi marw; a'r cwbl a wneir gan haneswyr, yn gyffredin, yw crybwyll ychydig am danom yn yr oesau gynt.'* (Our place in history has been denied us. We are viewed as a dead nation; and all that historians do, in general, is tell a little about us in ages long gone.)[58]

R.J. Derfel had drawn up a programme of practical measures calculated to stiffen Welsh resolve and engender a vigorously healthy sense of worth, but he knew for sure that the battle for self-esteem would only be won in the Welsh mind. External factors were, and still are, quite simply that – external; external to the crucial issue of how the Welsh think of themselves. The Lord Tonypandy bleat – 'What will *they* think of us?' – was ever the bleat of evasion and self-deception. Derfel's challenge to his compatriots in 1855 is every bit as relevant to the 'Welsh condition' at the beginning of the twenty-first century. And we should note that Derfel issued it not only in the aftermath of the 'Blue Books' assault, but in the afterglow of the Great Exhibition of 1851 when millions came to the Crystal Palace to wonder at England's might, and in the dazzle of hero-worship 'in excelsis' following the epic funeral of Wellington, the Great Duke, in 1852, and the publication of Tennyson's sweeping eulogy, 'The Charge of the Light Brigade', in 1854. This was his challenge:

> *Gymry! mae eich dyrchafiad a'ch enwogrwydd cenedlaethol yn gorphwys arnoch chwi eich hunain. A fynech chwi fod yn fawr ac enwog? Byddwch felly. Nid oes neb na dim a ddichon eich lluddias. Mae y moddion yn gyrhaeddadwy i chwi. Mae enwogrwydd yn dal coronau anrhydedd yn ei llaw, yn barod i'w rhoddi ar eich pen, ac os hebddynt y byddwch, arnoch chwi y bydd y bai.* (People of Wales! your advance and national fame depend on you alone. Do you wish to be great and famous? Be so. There is nothing and no one to prevent you. The means are within your reach. A myriad voices urge you forward. Fame holds the crowns of honour in her hand, ready to be placed on your heads, and if you are to be without them, you will only have yourselves to blame.)[59]

Should Wales fail to make its mark on the world's stage, its failure would be attributable not to material poverty, but to spiritual feebleness, want of moral fibre and a shameful disregard for the national, cultural legacy: *'Dysgwn barchu ein hunain, ac fe gawn barch gan ein cymdogion.'* (Let us learn to respect ourselves, and we shall be respected by our neighbours.)

It is as a response to R.J. Derfel's challenge that Owen Rhoscomyl's writings on Welsh history, as well as his script for The National Pageant in 1909, are best understood. He was, above all, concerned to combat *'yr ysbryd anwladgarol ag sydd beunydd yn dibrisio ac yn iselhâu gwlad ein genedigaeth'* (the unpatriotic spirit that is for ever depreciating and putting down the land of our birth). His historical romances, and his researched studies such as *Flame-Bearers of Welsh History* (1905) and *The Matter of Wales* (1913), were intended to arouse in the Welsh an awareness of a past characterized by heroic endeavour. That their forefathers had fought and lost against insuperable odds had not in any way destined their descendants to live their lives as 'born losers'. People throughout history had been defeated in wars by superior armies, but not until they surrendered their own story for that of the conqueror, and settled for a counterfeit identity, did they merit description as a cowed, inferior people. The Welsh had to regain a hold on their history and for that to happen they needed heroes, and accounts of heroic deeds, to inspire them.

The nineteenth century was a remarkable time for hero-worship in England. Alfred the Great, Cromwell, Nelson, Wellington, General Havelock, Livingstone, Gordon of Khartoum – the English had so many opportunities to celebrate their 'pre-eminence' among the nations of the world. And in Thomas Carlyle's *On Heroes, Hero-Worship and the Heroic in History* (1841) they had the most influential advocate for the role of the hero in the construction and maintenance of a nation's self-worth. There is no doubting Rhoscomyl's susceptibility to the magnetism of the heroic and it comes as no surprise to read in one of his daughter's, Olwen's, letters, that General Gordon's portrait hung on the wall of their home and that somehow his Bible and signet ring, too, had come into her father's possession. Following the publication in 1909 of Howell T. Evans's well-received *A History of England and Wales. From the Earliest Times to 1485*, Rhoscomyl would have been doubly impressed that the talented historian, in the course of an article on 'Llywelyn Bren' for *The Nationalist*, in January 1900, had made his case for the commemoration of heroes:

> Heroes are a national asset. The masses are born, live, die, and are no more. Heroes live on; and it is they who are thrown into the scales which estimate the moral and intellectual worth of a people.[60]

What Rhoscomyl most wanted was a change of image for his countrymen based on an appreciation of the fact that the Celts in their history had, unquestionably, been warrior people, and it was the persistence of a warrior spirit that had enabled the Welsh to contribute so worthily to the creation and expansion of the British Empire – a contribution that had never been properly acknowledged in England, let alone rewarded. It was as a warrior – a keyword in Rhoscomyl's nationalist lexicon – that he saw himself and it was in the hope of re-invigorating a warrior spirit in Wales that he wrote his adventure stories, his articles and books on Welsh history, and in 1909 scripted a National Pageant. He detested what he described as 'The mist-wreathed, moon-struck, fish-backed "Arnold-Renan" type' of Celt, a Celt concocted of poesy and magic. Rhoscomyl promoted instead his combative type and thundered that: 'The world always has been and always will remain the property of the successful warriors.' The 'Young Celts' he dismissed as war-decrying decadents who had taken for their spiritual father a Belgian dramatist – almost certainly Maeterlinck – who was the product of a nation without imperialistic ambition. What, one wonders, would H.M. Stanley, who served King Leopold in the hell that was the Belgian Congo, have had to say about that?[61]

THE WARRIOR SPIRIT

Rhoscomyl, while tracing the roots of his warrior Celt to the distant past, could also vouch for him as a living presence in contemporary Wales. He was no figment of the imagination; he was incarnate in Rhoscomyl himself, as he set about demonstrating in *Old Fireproof*, in which the strengths of 'the Captain' are those of his creator writ large. At the beginning of the novel the chaplain, who acts as narrator, is asked: 'Tell us, then, is the man of these times a fit or a degenerate descendant of them that carved our name so high and so far across the world?' And he replies, with 'Old Fireproof' in mind: 'The old race is not ended yet; we are not a folk full-spent, nor shall be soon, God still helping us.' He was such a one whose name 'connoted all that God intended when He said, "Let us make man" . . .', and he had an unshakeable faith in battle as the testing ground of a nation's pride and greatness: 'Battle wielders are the supreme lords of earth under God. The ultimate measure of a nation's strength and standing in the world is but the measure of its strength in the day of battle.' This is the Rhoscomyl whose prurient appreciation of the Gatling gun positively simmered. It is also Rhoscomyl in full agreement with J.A. Froude's imperialistic dictum that nations incapable of defending themselves are not fit for self-government.[62]

In the light of that conviction, a nation's youth couldn't learn too soon how to acquit themselves on the battlefield, couldn't identify too quickly with the honour and glory of warfare, couldn't immerse themselves in the heroic feats of their forebears too early on in life. R.J. Derfel in 1855 decried the fact that Welsh schoolchildren were not taught their country's history – it was for him one of the most bitter, most shaming causes of Welsh self-rejection. Rhoscomyl seized upon the same point when writing about 'Bosworth Field' in 1908, noting how very little Welsh history had been taught at all until recently, 'except according to English notions of it'. And in February 1909, when he addressed the Manchester Welsh National Society on 'Some outlines of the history of the Cymric race', he raged against the memory of being taught English history and told that he belonged 'to an inferior race, to a nation of conquered fugitives'. As a schoolboy he had refused to believe the lie and wanted the Welsh schoolchildren of 1909 to reject it as forcefully as he had done: 'My father and yours were not the cowards the English "history" says they were.' He would have the youth of Wales hear the truth about their national history and be emboldened by their appreciation of a heroic past. For him 'Youth!' was the hallmark of 'The Celtic Temperament'; the Celt needed no apologist support: 'He of all men should be all hope, since the strength is just beginning to pulse through his veins again. He is just feeling his feet once more, and in the race for place he may well breast out first, since he has youth on his side, and youth is the best half of the battle in any long struggle.' Wales as a 'young' nation of splendid potential excited Rhoscomyl, and he saw history as a means of revealing untold possibilities and of empowering his countrymen with a vision of their past to inspire their future.[63]

Flame-Bearers of Welsh History, published in 1905 when Evan Roberts's religious 'Revival' was certainly bringing some into the light and just as certainly pitching others into a lasting bewilderment, was also about revivalism – and about catching them young. The illustrated school edition – there were four colour pictures! – could be described as a recruitment drive among Welsh boys, the warriors of the future, the opening sentence of the Preface asserting that: 'No Welsh boy can well read the history of his ancestors – so stirring a record of so stubborn a race, such a good, grim, fighting race – without feeling that it is good to be a Cymro.' And once convinced of that he would go on: 'to feel that it is good to be a Briton, too, claiming a share in the glory of that crown and kingdom which was first founded by Cunedda the Burner, who was founder, too, of the Cymric nation.' It was Rhoscomyl's purpose in writing the book to ensure that: 'No Welsh boy need ever again go to the history of other peoples for a record of stirring deeds and struggles.'[64]

From the earliest beginnings to 'Victory and Fulfilment' following the Welsh-inspired victory on Bosworth Field, in forty-six brief chapters detailing the exploits of a rich assortment of battling heroes – Gwenllian of Kidwelly included, as she had the heart of a fighting man befitting the daughter of Gruffudd ap Cynan – Rhoscomyl told his story, ending on a triumphant note of assurance. It had been a proud thing to be a 'Cymro' in the glorious days of Elizabeth I. It was still so in 1905:

> It is a proud thing still to be a Cymro. Look back on all that your ancestors did and suffered in the centuries you have been reading of, and you will see how proud a heritage it is to be descended from such a race of splendid fighters for the right.[65]

He was also at pains to emphasize that leaders were only as good as the people they led. A prince could only do noble things at the head of a people if they, too, were on the side of noble things and prepared to fight and suffer for nobility. As in the past, so at the beginning of the twentieth century: 'the man who is most passionately answered, and most closely followed, is the one who sets the noblest aim before him, or who calls the people to the stubbornest struggle for the right, and the greatest sacrifice for lofty ideals'.[66]

That Rhoscomyl aspired to be that man for his Wales is certain. It was what compelled him to form the 'Welsh Horse' and caused him so much hurt when the command was denied him. All his urging and striving stemmed from his belief that: 'The old blood still stirs to the right call, whenever a leader with the old fire and the old tenacity appears.' In *Old Fireproof* the chaplain describes the first impression 'the Captain' made on him and we need not doubt that his words are true to Rhoscomyl's image of himself:

> Handsome was the first thing that I marked . . . though it was a handsomeness that had as a distinction the large, long eye one may see in medieval pictures. For, over all, handsome as he was, yet the one dominant note of him was mental strength, a mentality that was all one will to prevail like the molten steel

which, splashing from the furnace cauldron, burns its way relentlessly along its course, be that course straight or winding.[67]

'Old Fireproof' in death wished only to find the old leaders ready to acknowledge him 'as being of the old blood and the old name' – a Cymro who had been 'true to follow the right'. Rhoscomyl's short article on 'The Place of Wales in the Empire', published in *Wales* in 1912, made great play of the opportunities presented to the Welsh to act as leaders. A nation few in numbers could nevertheless lead. It was spiritual strength that mattered:

> For what makes the leader? What but high inspiration, clear vision, right purpose, and unswerving tenacity. And whence should such things come if not from our own land, waking from the neglect of centuries now that our young men may see that the field is set for them too, as well as for the rest, in the daily struggle of the Empire.

It was a simple matter of determination to lead, not follow, and to make Wales 'a breeding-place of leaders'. The nation's future would lie with young men 'seeing that the world is led by the men who had chiefly their own souls for weapons in the fight' and that 'some of the best and bravest are men of our own old race, the race of "never surrender".' [68]

Flame-Bearers of Welsh History, in the intensity of its desire to call schoolchildren to arms for the realization of Rhoscomyl's ambitions, has a Bismarkian ring to it. There is no mistaking its intent. In *Old Fireproof* there is a disturbing passage where 'the Captain' tells the chaplain of his vision, and of his joy in having already 'committed' his newborn son to its fulfilment. He had '[a] vision of all the work that I may do for men: all the wrongs that I may help to right: all the injustices that I may fight to overthrow'. Here is the chivalrous knight armed to the teeth with righteousness – and primed for regular blood-letting. A nation roused for truth and right, that would 'not brook wrong or injustice done, either at home or abroad' – that would be a nation to fight for:

> God! how splendid it would be to be a soldier then: a captain in an army that such a nation would send out on such an errand: how splendid to die, when one must, on such a field as one could fight if one were fighting in such a war as that! Aye! let us rouse our people to such a pitch again, and it would be something to thank God for to be alive then and turn its eyes on this wrong and that, and sweep the world clean of the greater evils.[69]

The whole of Europe would very soon resound with such pealing, delusive urging and its youth would drown in its spittle. The testimony of the Great War poets of 1914-18 drums in one's ears on hearing 'the Captain' recount how he had first seen his newborn son lying in the crook of his mother's arm:

> And I kissed her, and I thanked God, and I took down my carbine and bayonet that hung on the wall above the bed, and I laid the steel across his little hands and he was true: the little fingers gripped the steel and held fast while I lifted him half out of his mother's arms. 'Gwell angeu nag ovn,' I said. 'Better death than fear.'[70]

The little one was instantly true to fourteen hundred and fifty years of commitment, but he was also to inherit his father's vision and follow 'the true dawn' as seen by him. He would, of course, in accordance with 'the old Welsh laws' be trained if need be to fight for his country, 'taught and trained to war, that he may the better follow this greater vision, for he will know that, when it comes to the steel for it, he can take the steel with the best and worst of its enemies'.

Soon after 'the Captain' is mortally wounded, 'dying to keep faith with men . . . dying to save even the Kaffir that trusted him and came to him for help'. In his final moments the sergeant-major hears him whisper in Welsh: 'I'm not beaten! I'm dead, but I'm not beaten! And I have a son – and my wife knows – and she understands – she's splendid. I've never failed a trust – never given in – she won't; she's God's making . . . My son! – the vision – let him follow the vision – all his life – the vision!' It only remained then to bury him on the Spitzkop, the sergeant-major 'making magic on the grave so the Kaffirs from the kraal wouldn't meddle with it'. Afterwards the doctor said that God would get from him a clear report on how he found the world and how he left it:

> And the Lord God will look at him, and give him the nod, and say, 'Right, Captain! It seems quite clear; and now you'd better rest awhile till I call you.' And he'll salute and go, straight as steel, and quiet as steel, and he'll sleep sound, for he knows his honour is brighter than steel is sometimes kept.[71]

What a fearless and fearsome man Owen Rhoscomyl was. As uncompromising as a bayonet charge, he always saw his way forward clearly on all fronts and fully expected to be followed unquestioningly. Saving his life was not, for 'Old Fireproof', a soldier's chief concern. His primary purpose was to save his soul in doing his duty by his fellows and honouring the code of war. That is what Dai St John, the one-time Resolven bare-knuckle pugilist and Army heavyweight champion did at the battle of Belmont on 23 November 1899 when, charging with the Grenadier Guards, he bayonetted eleven of the enemy to death and was found after the assault 'shot through the brain, with his bayonet clean through a

DAI ST. JOHN

Boer's heart'. Dai St John, although their paths in South Africa do not seem to have crossed, was a Rhoscomyl warrior through and through who, in death, at the age of twenty-eight, was said to have won popularity to match that of Lord 'Old Bobs' Roberts himself.[72]

A National Pageant infused with that kind of spirit was what Rhoscomyl wanted to present to the people of Wales, a Pageant that over and above everything else had to be a success 'in its higher object of influencing the race – yes, the race'. Rhoscomyl had committed himself to discharging a great 'race-responsibilty', knowing that if the Pageant achieved its true purpose it would stir such pride in Welsh history as to create a desire to know more of it, 'and to read it with such sympathy as should seize upon its one magnificent lesson of "Never give in: keep fighting!", seize and absorb it to a fruitful future.'[73]

Rhoscomyl was sure that what he and G.P. Hawtrey, together with their cast of 5,000 players, were about to present would be an unforgettably vivid experience for the spectators. It should not be missed:

Come then and join your eyes to ours and see: come! – for 'The Honour of Wales' – come!

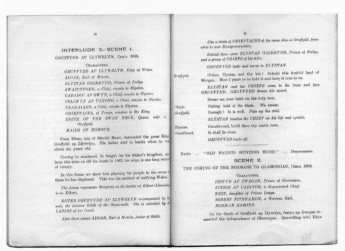

THE SCRIPT AS SET OUT IN THE *BOOK OF THE WORDS* BY G.P. HAWTREY AND OWEN RHOSCOMYL

LADY ST DAVIDS AS 'THE LADY OF DYVED'

'THE GREATEST EVENT IN THE ANNALS OF WALES'

RHOSCOMYL APPEARED before the appointing body for the post of Deputy Pageant-Master and Historian boosted by Sir Marchant Williams's extravagant estimation of his scholarship. Not, it would appear, that he was ever assailed by doubts about his competence. During the Boer War, Major Rankin recalled remarking in the course of a discussion that Wales had yet to find her historian. Rhoscomyl replied that there were only three men alive capable of writing a history of Wales. Rankin named (Sir) John Rhŷs and O.M. Edwards, his old tutor at Oxford, as two of them. Whereupon Rhoscomyl said: "'[y]ou are perfectly right . . . and the third is myself."' Rankin, in the course of discussing the occasional 'abstruse historical point' with him became 'more and more astonished at the appalling profundity of the man's erudition'. The somewhat incongruous adjective could be said to accord with Rhoscomyl's all-conquering attitude to life in general. Acquiring knowledge was also a matter of all-out attack for him.[1]

After Rhoscomyl returned to Wales at the end of the Boer War and eventually made his home in Dinas Powys, such of his papers as have survived refer to his 'historical researches', and his friendship with J. Glyn Davies stemmed from his visits, after 1907, to the National Library of Wales in Aberystwyth when Davies worked there. But in the absence of evidence there is no way of knowing how, before then, he had acquired the knowledge that 'appalled' Rankin. How much history had he read? And who were the historians who influenced him? Given the readiness and pungency of his opinions, his reticence with regard to his scholarly pursuits is regrettable. Had he written about Welsh historiography and how he proposed to contribute to its development, we would be better placed to comment on his appreciation of the historian's craft.

A letter Rhoscomyl wrote to O.M. Edwards, 4 February 1909, gives reason to believe that he saw himself treading in Edwards's footsteps. He sought the brilliant Oxford-educated historian's permission to add his name to an application for a Civil List pension he had been encouraged to make by David Lloyd George, MP, and Sir Marchant Williams. He then went on to say that he had accepted the post of historian for The Welsh National Pageant, having first satisfied himself that it had a sound chance of 'being National really' and a success 'both artistically and financially'. With characteristic Rhoscomyl bravura he declared himself satisfied 'that it's going to be the biggest thing in Pageants that this Isle of the Mighty has yet seen', and he had consequently 'taken on the Historian's job heart and soul'. He further counselled Edwards:

O.M. Edwards

88

Keep your eye on that pageant. There'll be such a burst of demand for Welsh history in Welsh schools as will gladden your heart after it's over. As I'm a sort of a disciple of yours, you'll feel that you've got a finger in that pageant by deputy.[2]

Rhoscomyl was denied a pension. What Edwards's reply was is unknown. That he was firmly committed to a proper and enthusiastic teaching of Welsh history in the schools and colleges of Wales is certain. But whether he was sure of Rhoscomyl's fitness for a missionary role in that field is open to question. It has to be said that the absence of any comment, appreciative or otherwise, on the National Pageant in Edwards's notable periodical, *Cymru*, is baffling, given that its very purpose was to enthuse a large readership with knowledge of the geography, history, language, literature and general culture of Wales as seen through the eyes of a romantic patriot.

It is tempting to surmise that O.M. Edwards, having published *Wales* in 1901 as an exemplary single-volume popular history of his country, felt a little 'chagrin' as Rhoscomyl in 1905 galloped on to the field astride *Flame-Bearers of Welsh History*, spurred on by Professors John Rhŷs and Kuno Meyer. For whatever reason, Edwards's *A Short History of Wales* appeared in 1906, and interestingly his name did not feature among those benefactors Rhoscomyl thanked at the end of his 'Introduction' to the 'Public Edition' of his book, whereas Rhŷs, 'first and principal' among them, together with Meyer, contributed a complimentary 'Preface', praising Rhoscomyl's intent and original methodology based on a scrupulous investigation of the old Welsh genealogies.

Professor John Rhŷs thought Rhoscomyl well prepared by the battle-scarred life he had led to write a history that was 'largely the story of wars and devastation', and to write it in a narrative style that would sweep young readers along with him. As 'an earnest and daring seeker after the truth in history', he would put his study of Welsh genealogies to scholarly use, aiming 'at reducing to an exact science what has only too often been given over to rhetoric and exaggeration'. His views, naturally, would not go unopposed and it was certain that Rhoscomyl would defend them – as he would also yield them up if convinced of their waywardness. For he had, Rhŷs believed, a true scholar's conscience. As for his patriotic intent, it was clear that his primary purpose was:

> to show broadly and clearly that the Cymry are not descended from a race of hares ready to run away at the first approach of an enemy, that on the contrary they were always ready to fight and to fight obstinately even when the numbers arrayed against them were overwhelming.[3]

And John Rhŷs, the first occupant of Oxford University's Chair of Celtic Studies, who returned to Wales at the end of the 1860s in the full flush of self-assurance as a meritorious Oxford graduate to announce the inevitable early demise of 'the dear, old Welsh language', was not about to underplay the 'British' significance of Rhoscomyl's achievement:

> There is no rebellious spirit abroad in the Principality, not even a clamour for home-rule; but on the other hand the true lover of human progress is deeply interested in seeing Welsh nationality develop to the full all that is best and noblest in it, rather than be forced into slavish imitation of the Saxon and the least progressive element in the composition of the great English people. That development could not help making him both a better man and a better citizen of the mighty Anglo-Celtic Empire, in which the accidents of peace and history have made him a piece of the mosaic, and with which his own setting and loyalty have insolubly identified him for ages past.[4]

It must have been very flattering for Rhoscomyl to have his efforts so warmly commended by Rhŷs, who had been on a pedestal in Wales ever since his epiphany as an Oxford professor in 1877. But how, one wonders, did the warrior who was soon to forecast the passing of Welsh 'timidity' in the face of English overlordship accommodate Rhŷs's well-tailored deference? It has to be that Rhŷs won him over with his vision of a true-to-himself Welshman becoming, for that very reason, 'a better man and a better citizen of the mighty Anglo-Celtic Empire'. A Wales rid of 'slavish imitation of the Saxon', in the van of an 'Anglo-Celtic Empire': Rhoscomyl would have found such a vision irresistible.

In this context it is worth remarking that John Rhŷs, O.M. Edwards, and John Morris-Jones, all three subsequently knights of the realm, distinguished themselves as Oxford scholars when 'Teutomania' flourished in England. For such leading Welsh 'Britishers' who had suffered a surfeit of 'Teutomongering', Rhoscomyl's admittedly unrestrained promotion of the Welsh Celt as an imperial asset must have afforded some relief. Both Edwards and Morris-Jones would deploy the Welsh language in their role as anti-Hun propagandists when the Kaiser went to war against their Anglo-Celtic Empire in 1914. Indeed, in his short-lived periodical, *Wales*, Edwards had already in 1895 spurned the 'intense patriotism' of historians such as J.R. Green and E.A. Freeman, dismissing Green's work as something fashioned by 'Teutonic patriotism, the most unhistorical the world has seen . . .', and likewise Freeman's, fashioned by 'a baseless sentimental patriotism, – an adoration of what he described in his books as the imaginary "forefathers" of the English people, and of what he described in conversation sometimes towards the end of his life as a "beery, boozy lot" . . .'5

As for John Morris-Jones, he produced a pamphlet, *Apêl at y Cymry: Mynnwn Germani ar ei Gliniau* (1914), an 'Appeal to the Welsh' in which he insisted on bringing Germany to its knees; he proclaimed the British Empire a power in defence of everything the Welsh held dear – freedom, justice and especially the rights of small nations; and he forcefully reminded his countrymen of their 'honourable place' in the Empire they had played no small part in founding and for which he fully expected them to fight against its enemies – thereby defending everything that was most sacred to them as a nation. It was doubtless their wish to advance the Welsh claim on British approval that prompted John Rhŷs to write all his scholarly works in English and John Morris-Jones, while he was Professor of Welsh at Bangor University College, to teach his students, up to his retirement, in the 'imperial tongue'.[6]

In his contribution to the 'Preface' of *Flame-Bearers*, Professor Kuno Meyer contented himself with encouraging remarks about Rhoscomyl's original use of genealogical studies as he set about elucidating Welsh history. He believed Rhoscomyl was developing a method of study 'based on truly scientific lines' and he saw 'a new field of investigation' opening up, 'promising a rich harvest'. Indeed, Meyer was optimistic that 'with the aid of philology and archaeology it will produce results more certain than those hitherto obtained', but he thought it too soon to judge whether Rhoscomyl's researches had yielded valid new insights in *Flame-Bearers*. There was need for 'much further investigation' and he could only hope that at a future date Rhoscomyl would be able 'to lay his researches before the public, in a still fuller (and more strictly scientific) manner'.[7] Notwithstanding his supportive tone of voice, Professor Kuno Meyer awaited further proof of the soundness of Rhoscomyl's conclusions. We still do so.

Despite O.M. Edwards's unexpected silence in the face of Rhoscomyl's *Flame-Bearers* and the National Pageant, their relationship seems to have been mutually appreciative. On his death, Edwards spoke warmly of Rhoscomyl's honourable and courteous disposition. He sensed something strange in his life story, but knew him to be as brave as a lion and as kind as a child, a loyal and energetic man who loved Wales passionately. It was at the National Eisteddfod held in Rhyl in 1904 that Rhoscomyl first made a powerful impression on Edwards, when his attention was drawn to a forthright character remonstrating with some English people who were noisily displeased with a platform speech in Welsh.[8] It was a significant visit for Rhoscomyl as he found in the presidential addresses of William Jones, MP, and David Lloyd George, MP, strong encouragement for his own views on the need to use history and drama to reinvigorate the national life of Wales.

Seeing and hearing him 'in action' describing the battle to come for Welsh rights, O.M. Edwards related to him as an author of historical romances and Hentyesque adventure stories who, in 1900, had sent him a scribbled Welsh war poem, set to the tune of 'The March of the Men of Harlech' by Taff Roberts, one of the Rimington Scouts. Rhoscomyl had forwarded it in a letter written when in the saddle, before Kroonstad, awaiting the order to attack. Edwards's acknowledgement in *Cymru*, to the effect that there is something uplifting and sanctifying in sacrifice for noble ends, would have much pleased the warrior who insisted that a soldier should go into battle intent, not on keeping his life, but on saving his soul. And he would have fully concurred with Edwards's view that should the end of the Boer War simply see Africa inundated with Chinese labour, prepared to work for less pay than a white or black man to further enrich German and Jewish millionaires, then many a father would feel that the life of a dear son had been sacrificed in vain.[9]

By the time Rhoscomyl's *The Matter of Wales* appeared in 1913, O.M. Edwards could take a cool look at his methodology, noting that he (I translate): 'puts his faith in the genealogies of the princes and promises much enlightenment by them. It is obvious that there is nothing unreasonable in his theory, and there is need of much patient investigation along the pathways he opens.'[10] The central argument of the book had already been outlined in the 'Introduction' to *Flame-Bearers of Welsh History*. It was that 'Y Cymry' had not been driven into Wales from their lands in west Britain by the conquering Saxons and Angles. They did not start their splendid story as losers and fugitives. On the contrary, they originated as a tribe from the 'Old North' (around Strathclyde in Scotland) led by Cunedda and his family, who set about reconquering those lands in the west taken by the

Saxons. It is vintage Rhoscomyl warrior-worship, written as if he had a premonition that very soon tens of thousands of Welshmen would be fighting for their Empire in a World War without precedent in human history.

It was a confident historian who set about scripting a National Pageant in 1909. His *Flame-Bearers,* sandwiched between O.M. Edwards's *Wales* (1901) and Professor J.E. Lloyd's *Outlines of the History of Wales* (1906) for use in schools and colleges, was not disregarded. Edwards's reputation was already firmly established, while Lloyd would soon cement his as 'the founding father of Welsh history written in the modern vein' with the publication of his magisterial *A History of Wales* in 1911. If Rhoscomyl felt challenged by such academic distinction, it wasn't apparent when he asserted that: 'Art may call from what lone heights of grandeur it will, it is the fiddler in the market place that folk will go on listening to.'[11]

Furthermore, as his presentation of 'The New Evidence' in the bold 'Introduction' to his *Flame-Bearers of Welsh History* made clear, he was convinced of the valid use he was making as a historian of the genealogies of the princes. He knew that he had found a tool with which to unlock the past in a way no one had done before, for those genealogies, as understood by him, were the equivalent of legal documents in the light of which any evidence pertaining to the beginnings of the 'Cymry' had to be authenticated. It was what his study of the genealogies had revealed to him that emboldened him to claim that much of the matter of his 'little book' was 'totally new'.[12]

It is as well for the purposes of this book that it is not necessary to delve into Rhoscomyl's unfinished study of what his friend, Professor J. Glyn Davies, called 'those infernal pedigrees'. Suffice it to say that he had convinced himself of the discovery of a formula, as unswerving as a 'Law of Nature', that winnowed what was true and false in the historical evidence to which it was applied, and allowed him to claim for 'the story of the beginnings of British History' in the first part of his *Flame-Bearers* an unprecedented accuracy. In the 'Introduction' to The

National Pageant's *Book of the Words*, he explained how he realized, after years of collecting and comparing genealogies one with another, 'that each generation was roughly of equal length.' It meant, for example, that descendants of the ninth generation from Cunedda were contemporary – that they were alive at the same time. The evidence pointed to the 'fact' that the generations 'kept level, kept step the whole way down through the centuries', Rhoscomyl did not see it as his business to account for the phenomenon; he simply asked that it be recognized as 'a historical fact of the greatest importance'.[13]

It has to be said that no succeeding historian of early Wales has felt constrained to adopt his formula, let alone trumpet its apparent infallibility. Even Rhoscomyl had to admit that it was 'not easy' to explain without a long series of examples! But his faith in his 'discovery' was unshakeable:

> If it is true that these genealogies exist, and are trustworthy, and if it is true that the generations, from AD 380 down to AD 1600, are contemporaneous, it follows that it is possible to establish roughly the date of any person of importance, whose name is mentioned in the records.[14]

He expected there to be some who would doubt 'the universal truth of this law' (from 'phenomenon' to 'fact' to 'law' was a mere canter for Rhoscomyl). If so, he would await their proof, following careful investigation, of its waywardness. But in the meantime he and G.P. Hawtrey would construct a National Pageant on the secure foundations of his, Rhoscomyl's, 'ground-breaking' research and insights.

The condensed account of the Pageant proper that follows draws on the extensive coverage, in words and pictures, given it by *The Western Mail* and, to a lesser degree, by *The South Wales Daily News*. It also draws on the *Book of the Words* by Hawtrey and Rhoscomyl, as well as E.A. Morphy's exuberant *Pictorial and Descriptive Souvenir*. It will attempt to conjure up something of the excited sense of high purpose felt in the blood by so many pageanteers during that summer fortnight in 1909 when Welsh history disported itself in Sophia Gardens, and by and large there will be no meddling with the facts as they were then presented, no querying of dates, no correcting of misspelt place names and no chiding of a fallible nomenclature (for example, today's Owain Glyndŵr will remain the anglicized and uncircumflexed Owen Glyndwr). But in trying to visualize things 'as they were', it will sometimes prove too difficult to resist the temptation of seeing their significance in the light of our today. For any sin of intrusion may a writer be forgiven.

Before 26 July when the Pageant fortnight officially commenced, Rhoscomyl and Edward Thomas (Cochfarf) had been about in south Wales canvassing support in both languages for 'the great venture'. They urged people to play their part in boosting an image of Wales as a country fit for a prominent place among the nations of the Empire. They implored parents to bring their children with them, so that in years to come they would recall the first awakening of pride in their homeland. Highlighting the educational aspect of the Pageant, Howell T. Evans, teacher, historian and member of the cast (he acted as understudy for Mr Rhys Williams, Miskin Manor), wrote letters to the press in Welsh and English stressing the 'truth' of the history they would see enacted. And it was pedagogical zeal, fully supported by Cardiff's Chief Inspector of Schools, Mr Isaac Vaughan Evans, himself an enthusiastic pageanteer, that brought some 90,000 schoolchildren to the three afternoon dress rehearsals staged for them from Tuesday to Thursday 20-22 July. On Tuesday, as many as 20,000 Cardiff children east of the Taff attended; on Wednesday over 40,000

EDWARD THOMAS (COCHFARF)

children were present, the vast majority of them from outside Cardiff and district; and on a very wet Thursday afternoon another 30,000 turned up, some coming from Herefordshire, Caernarvonshire (Bangor), Breconshire, Monmouthshire, Carmarthenshire and West Glamorgan.[15]

On Saturday, 24 July, when the two final dress rehearsals were held in Sophia Gardens, *The Western Mail* featured one lengthy account of 'How the Pageant Grew' and another, under the heading 'Pressmen on the Pageant', detailing the response of the press to the previous day's rehearsal held for their convenience. The first showered praise on the preparations of the various subcommittees during six months of 'incessant and hard work', and was presented as 'A splendid record of Patriotic Action'. Out of the labours of an army of committed, talented, resourceful volunteers had come a Pageant that was '"facile princeps" in comparison with all other such undertakings, those in London not excepted'. Cardiff's National Pageant of Wales was no mere copy of what had been done elsewhere:

> The arena is almost twice as extensive as any hitherto mapped out elsewhere for pageantry plays; the stand accommodation is unparalleled in character; while the arrangements for the illumination of the whole ground during the night performances, which will be unique, are far and away the most elaborate ever attempted in Wales or in England in connection with similar movements.[16]

There was so much to enthuse about. Careful planning over six months had necessitated a weekly meeting of the executive to scrutinize the work of the subcommittees established to ensure that everything functioned as perfectly as possible. No one shirked his or her responsibility and nothing was left to chance. Publicity in the form of 'many hundreds of thousands of pictorial postcards, adhesive stamps, leaflets, programmes, postcards etc' had been far-reaching, resulting in railway and steamboat companies offering the public exceptional facilities to visit Cardiff on 'all lines of route' to the city.

The grandstand, at a cost of £4,000, had to be erected because a National Pageant merited the outlay, and likewise the executive could not stint on the lighting arrangements entrusted to Messrs J.B. Saunders and Company. A historical Pageant intended to light up the life of a nation had itself to be lit up in dazzling fashion:

> Over 3,000 incandescent lamps had been used for illuminating the castle and the trees in the grounds, whilst the stage – a most important part of the general scheme – is beautifully lighted by a row of fourteen electric flare lamps placed on the top of the grand stand, in addition to which there are five searchlights of 10,000 candle-power, which will enable the Master to sweep the whole ground from his box. These lamps are of sufficient power to throw rays of light for over a mile.

The all-important telephone system enabling G.P. Hawtrey to communicate with fourteen different points on the vast field of operations was installed by the National Telephone Company for a nominal sum, its workers volunteering to do the work in their own time. And the castle that Ivor Bach's men would storm in Episode 4 was built and painted in 'Pageant House', its drawbridge made to work by balance weights and chains so that it could be lowered exactly 'as in the olden days'.[17]

The great investment of time and effort made by so many individuals intent on ensuring a 'national triumph' was exemplified by Lord Mayor Lewis Morgan and his family, who took to pageanteering wholeheartedly. The Marchioness of Bute had given the patrician players a lead by turning out in all her splendour as 'Dame Wales' on a rainy afternoon so as not to disappoint the thousands of schoolchildren who had flocked to a dress rehearsal. It is true that not much was seen of her after the Official Opening on 26 July, the Wagner Festival in Bayreuth proving an irresistible attraction for the Butes, but her support was never in doubt. In her absence, her understudy Miss Moya Finucane scored a personal triumph, establishing herself as the

THE HEROINE OF THE HOUR: DAME WALES DEFEATS THE RAIN
(A Staniforth cartoon)

Pageant's darling in no time at all! The Reverend Evan Rees (Dyfed), the then Archdruid of Wales, and the Reverend Ifor Thomas, vicar of Aberpergwm, in their respective roles as Archdruid in Episode 1 and Dewi Sant in Interlude 2 were two other players whose loyal support, it was said, clearly illustrated the readiness of people seen as prominent figures in Welsh life to serve a colourful national cause.[18]

CITY OF CARDIFF.

To the Citizens of Cardiff and the Inhabitants of the District.

PROPOSED

WELSH NATIONAL & HISTORICAL

PAGEANT.

I, the undersigned, LEWIS MORGAN. Lord Mayor of the City of Cardiff, hereby give notice that a

PUBLIC MEETING

WILL BE HELD AT THE

CITY HALL, CARDIFF,

ON

THURSDAY, THE 14TH DAY OF JANUARY, 1909

AT EIGHT O'CLOCK P.M.

for the purpose of deciding upon the promotion of a WELSH NATIONAL AND HISTORICAL PAGEANT, to appoint a representative Committee to carry same into effect and to arrange all details in connection therewith.

All interested are most cordially invited to be present to support the Movement and lend every assistance in the organisation and promotion of a NATIONAL PAGEANT worthy of the Principality.

LEWIS MORGAN, Lord Mayor.

CITY HALL, CARDIFF, JANUARY 5th, 1909.

WESTERN MAIL, LTD., CARDIFF.

THE CAST OF THE PAGEANT WAS BOOSTED BY NUMEROUS ANIMALS, INCLUDING
BLOODHOUNDS AND HORSES

Remarkable contributions were made, for example, by J.M. Staniforth, *The Western Mail*'s much loved cartoonist, who sketched the designs for some 40,000 pieces of costume; by Mrs T. Snead Davies, a former member of the Carl Rosa Company entourage who practically lived at 'Pageant House' for six months where, as 'Captain' of the hundreds of lady workers, she organized the making of the costumes; by Mrs Perkins, the 'Mistress of the Wardrobe', who bore responsibility for the distribution and safe return of the costumes; by Colonel Henry Lewis, Greenmeadow, and Councillor Edward Nicholl, chairman of the Horse Committee, who undertook to raise a troop of fifty horsemen and found in Mr E.P. Evans a veterinary surgeon to see to the proper care of the horses throughout; and by Mr Ernest George Cove, a Devonshire lad brought up in Treorchy from the age of ten and recently turned a professional actor after years of competing in 'eisteddfodau'. Having shed his long-held Nonconformist prejudice against the stage, Cove's enthusiasm for acting now knew no bounds. He took four parts in the Pageant, making a striking impression as the Scout in Episode 1 and as Shakespeare's 'Fluellen' in Episode 5, in addition to which he spent many hours training the various groups of amateur players for their parts. As a star pageanteer none better embodied the talent and vigour required to bring the crowds to life and involve them in the proceedings – crowd involvement for Louis Napoleon Parker being of the utmost importance – and Cove was rewarded for his efforts with shouts of approval and Hawtrey's appreciation.[19]

As for the 'herculean labours' of the treasurer, Mr J. Allcock, the secretary, Mr A.W. Swash, Rhoscomyl the historian and G.P. Hawtrey the pageant-master, *The Western Mail* of 24 July was as lavish in its praise as had been Raymond Blathwayt a month earlier. For Blathwayt, A.W. Swash was an organizational genius. Rhoscomyl, alias Vaughan, was 'a perfect marvel' who had 'the real history' of Wales at 'his finger-ends' and was about to bring the nation 'face to face with its wild and ancient self'. Without him, the pageant as 'a historical display would not be worth the paper upon which its story is inscribed', and to see him as Hawtrey's co-producer 'dashing about all over the ground, absolutely blazing enthusiasm into all and sundry' was to witness dynamism incarnate. What Hawtrey offered was 'the unconquerable determination and unquenchable vigour of the Master himself', who could turn a host of rugby footballers into 'the fierce, untamed Welshmen of the Middle Ages' and convince them that as pageanteers they would be playing for Wales exactly as if they were taking the field at the Arms

A.W. SWASH

Park: 'Remember, the whole of Wales, North and South, will be looking on. Be as serious at this as if you were playing in the Cup Final.'[20]

To be depicted again on the eve of the official opening of the Pageant as someone 'whose services to Wales have been inestimable', as a scholar who 'has drained almost every available source of information on Welsh historical facts', as a writer who 'has made every Welshman proud of the glorious history of his native land' and in exposing 'many fallacies in English historical text-books' and advancing facts 'creditable to his nation' yet hitherto ignored, thus giving his countrymen sound reason to stand tall – all this must surely have satisfied even Rhoscomyl's cormorant appetite for praise. Hawtrey was likewise praised anew for his grasp of detail, for his mastery of all aspects of staging a pageant, for refusing to be beaten by any unexpected problem, and for dealing with his huge cast 'with evenness of temper throughout'. And again, there was Secretary Swash, 'the "marvel" of the show', to salute for his untiring work, a man fit to be a top diplomat who had 'the energy of a Trojan'. How *The Western Mail* extolled them and rejoiced in their feats.[21]

When, at the end of June, the costumes had been finished and it was found that the Pageant was short of a thousand men to wear them, Rhoscomyl and Mr E.C. Willmott, the chairman of the Performers' Committee, undertook to visit 'all the offices at the Docks, all the engineering works, and every place where any number of men were employed . . . with the result that more than sufficient men were found to fill every place'. Employers were ready to assist wherever they went and when the final dress rehearsals were held on 24 July all parts were filled. Rhoscomyl was not easily refused.[22]

For Wednesday night, 23 June, Mr Isaac Jones of Brynna, concerned at the shortage of horseriders for the Pageant, organized an event to drum up support in the Vale of Glamorgan. Rhoscomyl and his wife, together with A.W. Swash and Edward Thomas (Cochfarf), travelled by train to Llanharan to lend their aid. They were met by several riders, including the egregious daughter of the late Dr William Price (1800-93) of Llantrisant, and proceeded to hold a demonstrative meeting on the village square under a fluttering Red Dragon. A rousing 'Hen Wlad Fy Nhadau' sent them on their way to Brynna accompanied by two dozen riders. Following another highly charged sequence of speeches and songs they made for Pencoed, with a cavalcade of at least 45 riders and a crowd of cyclists accompanying their wagonette. Hundreds of enthusiasts had gathered in Pencoed and 'cheered lustily the fine nationalist sentiments expressed by Owen Rhoscomyl and his supporters'. As a result a large number of riders, including Miss Price, enrolled for mounted parts in the Pageant, and many more applications from the Vale were expected to reach 'Pageant House' shortly. They were, indeed, heady times.[23]

And then on Friday 23 July the press came to pass judgement on what a dress rehearsal would reveal of The National Pageant's likely outcome. Did it merit the large claims made on its behalf? Quoting from *The Times*, *The Daily Graphic*, *The Daily Mail*, *The Liverpool Daily Post*,

The South Wales Daily Post, The Bristol Times and Mirror, The Western Daily Press, The Bristol Daily Mercury and *The Cambrian Daily Leader* under the heading – 'Pressmen on the Pageant' – *The Western Mail* further buoyed the optimism of the promoters as all the reports were decidedly favourable. Considered as a whole it was 'magnificent'; a 'very fine show indeed'; a 'most striking manifestation of public and patriotic spirit', the finale 'the most magnificent picture ever seen in Wales, and, probably, out of it'; 'Artistically, the Pageant is a pronounced success, and fine weather alone is needed to make it a financial one'; 'under clear skies and with the presence of general sunshine it will have an educational and inspiring influence the importance of which cannot be over-estimated'; 'of unique attractiveness, and, skilfully organized, it has already proved a conspicuously successful undertaking'; and, to Rhoscomyl's great satisfaction, no doubt, *The Cambrian Daily Leader* averred that Welshmen were able to relive their glorious past 'and to realise with a vividness that awakened a sense of pride the Cymry's contribution to the might of Britain'.[24]

Such comments, which were later handsomely supported by further reports in *The Times, The Morning Post, The Bristol Times and Mirror, The Evening Standard, The Daily Dispatch* and *The Daily Express* – *The Morning Post* putting the Pageant on a par with the Oberammergau Passion Play – were a tremendous fillip to everyone involved in 'the great venture'. *The Daily Graphic* and *The South Wales Daily Post* also served a useful purpose in focussing attention on the need to quicken the performance of the Pageant, a matter which Hawtrey promptly took in hand, highlighting the need for the performers in each and every scene to be properly marshalled and ready to play their parts without delay. That would be the responsibility of the 'Captains' appointed to act as marshals for each group of performers and Hawtrey made it clear that the smooth running, and ultimately the public enjoyment, of The National Pageant of Wales depended on their efficiency. Progress by fits and starts would be disastrous. By 26 July, Hawtrey had the running time down to the target duration of three hours, the episodes lasting between twelve and fifteen minutes, and the interludes between ten and twenty minutes. Bioscope pictures had been taken during the final dress rehearsals on behalf of the proprietors of the Cardiff Empire, to be shown in the Empires at Swansea and Newport as well and probably at the London Coliseum too. Everything seemed set fair for what would be in the true sense of the word a historic triumph.[25]

If the Pageant was to succeed, its spectacular, eye-widening appeal had to be established from the beginning, its emotional impact heightened by an imaginative use of music. And for *The Western Mail* the scene, as the Lord Mayor in his robes of bombazine and gold performed the opening ceremony, could not have been better despite the sparsely occupied shilling seats:

LORD MAYOR LEWIS MORGAN

Bright sunlight, with a glitter of gold and silver and the flash of many colours on a cool, green lawn. Never has a Pageant had so brilliant an opening as that of the National Pageant of Wales on July 26th. The events were in keeping with the day.[26]

THE LORD MAYOR RINGS UP THE CURTAIN

(A Staniforth cartoon)

THE MARCHIONESS OF BUTE AS 'DAME WALES'

Heralds sounded a fanfare, the band played, a choir sang 'The March of the Men of Harlech' as the Marchioness of Bute came out of the Castle in the guise of 'Dame Wales', accompanied by Edward German's 'Welsh Rhapsody'. And what a 'Dame Wales'! J.M. Staniforth must have chuckled to see his stout, folksy, wholesome cartoon country-woman transmuted into a 'Dame' fit to dazzle the nubile daughters of 'Cool Cymru' almost a century later:

> Lady Bute, as Dame Wales, wears a dress of eau-de-nil satin, richly embroidered in shades of blue and coral pinks, a large red dragon being emblazoned on the front of the skirt. The sleeves are of gold tissue edged [with] pearls, and over this garment is worn a robe of cloth of gold enriched with white velvet applique. Beautiful exceedingly are the jewels which Lady Bute wears, comprising a magnificent jewelled belt, with necklace, pendant, and bracelet en suite, very long gold earrings set, turquoise, diamond, and pearl bracelet, gold jewelled crown, from which hangs a long veil of gold tissue. Gold shoes are worn.[27]

She was followed by Lady Margaret Stuart bearing her full Court train, together with Lady Noah Noel and Miss Alice Naish as Ladies-in-waiting – the three, needless to say, attired in a fashion becoming the sumptuous appearance of the Marchioness.

Then came the thirteen 'ladies of high social distinction' representing the counties of Wales and Monmouthshire, each preceded by a standard-bearer and accompanied by bevies of fairies in their respective colours:

> Anglesey – Miss F. Herbert, Belgrave Square, London. Fairies in mauve and gold.
> Brecon – Mrs Oliver Jones, Fonmon Castle. Fairies in green and pink.

Cardigan – Miss Sybil Williams, St Donat's Castle. Fairies in terracotta and green.

Carmarthen – Miss May Davies, Cathedral Road, Cardiff. Fairies in brown and gold.

Caernarvon – Mrs Lawson Jones, Havelock House, Cardiff. Fairies in grey and pink.

Denbigh – Mrs Gilbert Heaton, Cathedral Road, Cardiff. Fairies in pink and green.

Flint – Mrs Snead Davies, Conway Road, Cardiff. Fairies in fawn and helio.

Glamorgan – The Lady Ninian Crichton Stuart. Fairies in red and cream.

Merioneth – Miss Nancy Ivor Williams, Dyffryn Ffrwd, Nantgarw. Fairies in blue and terracotta.

Monmouth – Mrs Waldron, Bluetts, Peterstone. Fairies in white.

Montgomery – Mrs Ivor Williams, Dyffryn Ffrwd, Nantgarw. Fairies in cream and gold.

Pembroke – Mrs Treharne, Coed-ar-hyd-y-glyn, Cowbridge. Fairies in two shades of blue.

Radnor – Mrs Tudor Crawshay, Dimlands, Llantwit Major. Fairies in blue and cream.

Wearing silver crowns and veils, and with the arms of the county represented emblazoned on each dress, the ladies were, not surprisingly, much admired. Lady Ninian Crichton Stuart, for instance, wore 'a green satin dress with white sleeves and silver trimming'. From her shoulders 'a cloak of silver-trimmed green satin ... hung – by silver chain ornaments', and accompanying her were 'dear little fairies in red frocks, apparently tied on with many ribbons and cream colour wing sleeves'. They came in procession towards the grandstand, in front of which some six to seven hundred schoolchildren, in a great burst of colours, came together in crescent formation to make their fairy dance 'a dream of Celtic phantasy and delight' as 'Dame Wales' prepared to set the Pageant proper in motion.[28]

The Lord Mayor of Cardiff - "Hywel Dda."	Viscount Tredegar - "Owen Glyndwr."
Lady Bute - - "Dame Wales."	Lord Mostyn "His Ancestor at Bosworth."
Lady Llangattock - -	The Archdruid of Wales "The Archdruid."
"Wife of Owen Glyndwr."	The Chief Constable of Glamorgan
Lady Ninian Stuart - "Glamorgan."	"Chief Ruffian."

REALISTIC ONSLAUGHT ON CARDIFF CASTLE

BY HUNDREDS OF EMINENT FOOTBALLERS.

MAGNIFICENT FIREWORK DISPLAYS

JULY 28th and 29th, by BROCK, of the Crystal Palace.

BAND OF THE ROYAL MARINES

Nothing like this Pageant has ever been seen in the Principality before.

PERFORMANCES:

JULY 26 to 31 at 2.30 p.m. AUGUST 2 to 7 at 7.30 p.m.

Two Performances on Saturday, July 31st and August 7th, and Bank Holiday 2.30 and 7.30.

THE EVENING PERFORMANCES WILL BE BRILLIANTLY ILLUMINATED BY **10,000** MOST POWERFUL ELECTRIC LAMPS, MAKING THE SCENE A PERFECT FAIRYLAND.

ADMISSION - 1/-

(STANDING ACCOMMODATION ONLY),

RESERVED SEATS :---10/6, 7/6, 5/- and 2/6

Booking Office---PAGEANT HOUSE, Wharton Street, CARDIFF.

Pageant Parade through the City
Dress of 'Dame Wales'

LADY NINIAN CRICHTON STUART
AS 'GLAMORGAN'

MRS TUDOR CRAWSHAY, DIMLANDS,
AS 'RADNOR'
(by permission of Miss S. Crawshay)

Calling on the counties of Wales to 'stand forth', with Monmouthshire no exception:

> For though great England claims thee for her own,
> Cymric thou art, and Cymric shalt remain.

she proceeds to explain the purpose of their gathering:

> . . . We have met to celebrate
> The mighty heroes of a bygone time;
> To show them as they lived, and fought, and died,
> And so to keep them fresh in memory.

Each county was to:

> Recall her heroes from the distant past,
> And thus in order bring them on the scene.

The counties, in true Welsh fashion, fall to bickering about their claims on various heroes, Owen Glyndwr in particular being the target of several claimants, whereupon 'Dame Wales' tells them to desist, as 'Glyndwr belongs to Wales'. She then orders them to disperse, sending Monmouth to find Caradoc:

> . . . Send him on,
> And let him grace our opening Episode.[29]

The first episode, circa 50 AD, for which the band plays Gounod's 'Hunting Music' as an overture, brings on Caradoc and his followers to seek an alliance with Rhys, the king of the Silures, 'a fierce, warlike people' respected for their fighting qualities by Tacitus. A scout, recognized by an animated spectator as a 'bachan o Dreorci' (a chap from Treorchy), locates the king (Mr Rhys Williams, Miskin Manor) with his hunting party, informs him of Caradoc's purpose, and is sent back to fetch him. The king, along with his chiefs, queen, Olwen (Miss Pinkerton, Llanishen), and her maidens, advances towards the grandstand to meet Caradoc (Mr Goodwin Preece, Cardiff) and his party of twelve led by the scout (Mr Ernest George Cove). As Caradoc advances, leaving a rearguard of nine, The Archdruid (Dyfed) enters accompanied by bards, ovates, trumpeter and swordbearer, all of whom stand near the king.

Caradoc is greeted as 'Noble Prince' and is asked to explain the purpose of his visit. He tells Rhys of his ongoing war against the Roman invaders who, despite many a check, still press forward, 'Westward, ever westward.' Now, having crossed the Severn, they are near at hand. Rhys commands the Archdruid to put the question – War or Peace? – to the people, which he does in fine eisteddfod style. The

Mr Goodwin Preece as 'Caradoc'

trumpeter sounds three blasts, and from all quarters, warriors, old men, women and children assemble before the Archdruid. Taking the sheathed sword he lifts it and holds it, true to Gorsedd practice, in a horizontal position. With four bards holding the sheath, he half draws the sword and cries, '*A Oes Heddwch?*' (Is there Peace?), only to be answered with a ringing uneisteddfodic shout – '*Rhyfel!*' (War!). The ritual is repeated twice more with the same result, following which the Archdruid unsheathes the sword in full and passes it to Rhys, who gives it to Caradoc with the words: 'It is war. Be thou our Avenger.' Caradoc responds: 'To the death.'

As the warriors put on the war paint, the scout hurries through Caradoc's rearguard to warn that the Romans are coming. At Caradoc's command, 'Silures – forward!', the warriors march off, whereupon Queen Olwen draws a knife and orders all the women, also wielding knives, 'Forward!' with them. With 'Amazonian impulse' they hurry to the slaughter, their shrieks intensifying the men's blood-lust.[30]

Seen as 'a most stirring spectacle' that got the Pageant off to a gripping start, *The Western Mail*'s 'Pageant Pictures' supplement entered into the spirit of the players:

In a moment the Silurian warriors, their spears gleaming in the sun, swept into battle array, and, followed by the women with knives unsheathed, and children glorying in the prospect of war, the host rushed off while the strains,

>   Let the hills resound with song
>   As we proudly march along,

flooded the air, making every responsive heart thrill with patriotic delight in the heroism of the ancient days.[31]

Again, the appearance of 'a primary-coloured crowd, mostly wearing bright reds, blues, and greens' fixed the spectators' attention. Rhys, the king of the Silures, wore a green *'pais'* or tunic and a purple cloak. Olwen, his queen, wore yellow with black decoration, and her long cloak was blue, with yellow decorations. Caradoc was 'a terrifying person of most barbaric appearance . . . his scarlet 'pais' or tunic decorated with three leopards' heads which, we are told, were of brass in old times and fashioned for defence as well as ornament (cf. Rhoscomyl's leopard claw when serving with the Rimington Scouts).

SILURIAN WARRIORS AND THEIR WIVES

The Archdruid, clothed in 'virgin white', wore a gold torque around his neck as 'an emblem of judicial power', and in his hand 'the crystal, the emblem of holiness and truth'.[32]

There was indeed incident and colour enough in the opening episode to delight the eye. A large cast, much movement and passion, a modicum of words – it all resulted in a kindled sense of anticipation in the crowd of onlookers. And for Rhoscomyl in particular the essential truth of his view of Welsh history was put centre stage at the outset – Caradoc in alliance with Rhys of the Silures leads a people's army against the forces of the mightiest empire the world had yet seen. Men and women motivated by patriotism and a hatred of tyranny rush to confront the Romans. They lose to superior forces of course, and as the *Book of the Words* tells us, Caradoc, betrayed by Cartismandua, queen of the Brigantes, is taken in chains to Rome where both his indestructible spirit of resistance and his nobility command the respect of the Emperor, Claudius, who spares his life. What follows in the Pageant is a celebration of that spirit at work throughout the ages until, as Rhoscomyl together with the vast majority of his countrymen believed, it triumphed on Bosworth Field in 1485 and in the subsequent Act of Union England and Wales became as one in an empire mightier than that of Rome.

In the interlude that follows, four quickly moving scenes depict the Romans laying the foundations of Cardiff, circa 60 AD, Maximus the Great proclaimed Emperor of Rome, 380 AD, Vorttigern bringing in the Angles to protect himself against Cunedda, 449 AD, and the first wave of the 'Cymry' settling in Wales, circa 475. The band sets the tempo by playing Beethoven's 'Quick March' for the first scene, George Miller's 'Harmonized Flourish' for the second and Pierné's 'Characteristic March' for the third. No words are spoken during the first and third scenes, and very few during the second and fourth, but they were 'depicted in silhouettes of exquisite pageantry.'[33]

The Emperor Maximus (Mr Morgan Davies, Whitchurch), an embodiment of the Roman 'pride of possession', stands out 'in a cotehardie of brilliant scarlet, gold cuirass, and Imperial mantle, accompanied by his mounted bodyguard.' He is seen addressing the representatives of the five peoples in Britain at that time – Romans, Britons, Saxons, Picts and Scots – with his six sons in attendance. A Roman military tribune, bearing the purple cloak, tells him that the Legions are tired of Gratian's rule and want him to lead them to victory: 'Be thou our Caesar.' Maximus is assured of the five peoples' support, 'Maximus! Maximus! Imperator!', and responds: 'If ye will follow me to Rome, I will take the purple and be your leader.' They shout: 'The Purple! Take it!' And so the King of Britain follows Caradoc to Rome – a conqueror soon to be Emperor.[34]

Nothing is said of Vorttigern's infamous recruitment of the Angles, under Hengist and Horsa, to help him withstand Cunedda's raids, nor of his marriage to Alis Vronwen (Rowena), an Anglian princess, to boot. It is as if the act that led eventually to the overthrow of the Britons is too shaming for words. But the coming of the first wave of 'Cymry' to settle in Wales, circa 475, restores the martial pace again. The sons of Cunedda, Einion Erth (the Bear), and Osmael (known as Gwron – the Hero) come down from Scotland to establish themselves on the peninsula where Llandudno now stands. Their sisters, Princess Gwen and Princess Tegaingl, want to settle there permanently, but Osmael wants to go to Anglesey where fresh hordes of Scots, coming over from Ireland, promise fine sport for a warrior. And so he goes, leaving Einion with their sisters in a land worth fighting for.[35]

E.A. Morphy wrote of Cunedda and his children with Hollywoodish excess – Cunedda is recalled as a Pictish king who 'made his fields a muck of blood before he harrowed them'. But in trumpeting 'the fact' that the two daughters of Sir Pyers Mostyn of Talacre, Miss C. Mostyn as 'Tegaingl' and Miss Agnes Mostyn as 'Gwen', proved a 'family survival' going back to the fifth century, Morphy excelled himself. Tegaingl was the reputed grandmother of King Arthur, named by Gildas as the 'Pagan Lioness of Devon', whose 'copper-hued tresses fell about her, in glory, like a mantle'. The Mostyn family descended in

THE MOSTYN SISTERS AS
'TEGAINGL' AND 'GWEN'

two lines from Tegaingl and Gwen, and Sir Pyers Mostyn 'from a genealogical point of view' was the head of the main direct branch of the family. And as proof of his family's unbroken descent from Cunedda his two daughters, like nearly all the fairest daughters descended from Tegaingl over the centuries, boasted the same 'wonderful copper-coloured tresses which fell in glory like a mantle around the "Pagan Lioness of Devon"'. Historians might disdain such 'evidence', but it was the very stuff of pageantry and made a great selling-point. Morphy was not about to pass up on any 'amazing resuscitations . . . from the greyer mists of antiquity', and in the two Mostyn sisters it was doubtful 'that all Europe could produce a more distinguished example of remote genealogy'.[36]

The second episode, circa 510 AD, enacts the crowning of Arthur (Mr R. Graham, Bute Road) by Merlin (Mr Ifano Jones, Cardiff Central Library's Chief Librarian), and in the *Book of the Words*, gave Rhoscomyl, the researcher, an opportunity to startle Tennyson's readers by informing them that the legendary King was a composite of three different men drawn from three main sources. Mallory's 'Morte d'Arthur' dealt principally with the great Arthur who was killed in 537 AD at the battle of Camlan 'against the second wave of the Cymry.' He belonged to Flintshire, 'where Camaloc still remains on the map'. The second Arthur, as revealed in Walter Map's 'High History of the Holy Grail', was the king of Dyfed who perished with the coming of the third wave of the 'Cymry', circa 580 AD. He was the Arthur associated with the quest for the Holy Grail, which Rhoscomyl knew to be 'a misreading and mistranslation' of 'Sang Real' = the Royal Blood, that is, the blood of Christ. Mistakenly rewritten as 'San Greal', 'sang' meaning 'blood' became 'san' meaning 'holy'. The third Arthur, associated with north-west Wales, died circa 635, having held his court 'as the Mabinogion say, at Gelli Wic in Cernyw (the peninsula of Lleyn)'. No matter how fanciful his three-in-one Arthur might have appeared to others, Rhoscomyl had no doubts, and, in the Pageant, Mallory's Arthur is crowned King of Tegaingl by Merlin, the Archdruid, during the funeral of King Cynvor in a field outside the High Hall of Camaloc.[37]

The mood is set for the episode as the choir sings the lament,

MERLIN CROWNS KING ARTHUR

'Morfa Rhuddlan', and the band plays a 'Solemn March' by George Miller as the funeral procession approaches the cromlech on the field in front of the grandstand. Arthur, handsome in scarlet with a blue cloak, steel armour and shield, enters 'carrying the spoils of a conquered prince', and makes for the cromlech. Merlin, the Archdruid, is followed by bards, ovates, trumpeter and a sword-bearer who carries 'the terrible blade-spear'. Before the assembled princes, spearmen, youths-in-training and wailing women, the sword-bearer places the blade-spear on the cromlech and Merlin challenges whosoever would be king to lift the blade of kingship.

Watched by Morwen Levani aka Morgan la Faye (Miss Lester-Jones, Llandough), Gwenuver (Mrs Robert Hughes, Sully) 'in crimson kirtle, green tunic, blue mantle, with much gold decoration and white wimple', together with her ladies and the wounded Lancelot, Merlin tries to persuade a very reluctant Arthur to be king: 'King? Not I, Merlin. What man would be a King if he might still be a free warrior? Nay let me be free.' He resists Morwen's attempt to break his warrior's will with thoughts of 'Splendour! Riches! Love!' – the prizes that all men seek – with a disdainful reply: 'Men! They are no men that love these things.' At this point Merlin alerts him to the ill designs of Black Yrien, takes the crown from the bier, flashes the stone in Arthur's eyes, and then places the crown by the blade on the cromlech. As Black Yrien reaches for the blade Arthur heeds Merlin's warning, turns, and seizing the blade plunges it through him. Without pause he issues his challenge: 'Which other of you will stand forth? Which other of you will be King over Arthur?' And they all turn away.[38]

Compared with Mallory's Arthur, the Arthur of the Round Table, of Camelot and the Holy Grail, Rhoscomyl's Pageant Arthur is hardly a figure of high romance. There is nothing chivalric in the killing and dismissal of Yrien: 'Carry him off. Take him and lay him with his fathers.' And when Merlin places the crown on his head, he immediately takes it off, tosses it to Gwenuver 'who is standing spellbound', and bluntly tells her: 'Take it. Something to play with. Now bear we Cynvor to burial, and then to battle ourselves.'

What Rhoscomyl wanted to impress upon the Pageant's onlookers was the warrior at the heart of Arthurian romance. It was a bred in the bone fighting man, one not to be deflected from his purpose by covetousness and easy living who, as legend had it, laid low mighty Rome itself and left for posterity an image of imperishable greatness. Rhoscomyl's Arthur, once convinced of the rightness of the course urged upon him, acts decisively, as Yrien finds to his cost, and goes on to achieve great things. He is the antithesis of that 'timidity' Rhoscomyl sought to rid his Wales of, and a mighty exemplar of the imperialistic spirit at work.

The second interlude is composed of four scenes. The first two mark the coming of the second and third waves of 'Cymry', circa 550-575 AD, and their early confrontations with Christianity. The third scene, no more than a silent procession of monks, signifies that the erstwhile independent 'Cymric Church' has submitted to the authority of the Church of Rome following the conversion of St Leuver (Lles) by Eleutherius, Bishop of Wessex, circa 675 AD. He, in turn, sets about converting the whole church, the change being accomplished by 778 AD when Elvod of Holyhead, following his conversion, is made Archbishop of Gwynedd. The fourth scene, circa 875 AD, bears witness to the significance of Rhodri Mawr (Mr D. Llewellyn Treharne, Pentre) and his seven sons. Rhodri Mawr was killed in 877 AD, leaving unfulfilled his ambition to unite Wales under one 'Over-king'. Preceded by a trumpeter and a herald who announce his coming together with his sons, they ride forward, 'a splendid squadron – galloping, "ventre à terre", to the call of the charge from the woods on the right of the grandstand'. They exit, leaving the onlooking thousands (as was hoped) to ruminate on the lost opportunities that loom large in the Welsh past.[39]

In the first scene, for which the band plays Batiste's 'Pilgrim Song of Hope', the 'Cymry' have lodged themselves after the death of Arthur in that part of Wales known as Ceredigion, so named after Ceredig (Mr H. Eyre, Court Road School), the foremost son of the second Cunedda. It is here, where paganism reigns, that the 'Cymric Church' takes root. Ceredig, as a pagan king, has his men capture a fleeing Christian, whereupon his priest insists that he be sacrficed to their gods. Gildas, a Christian teacher (Reverend R.R. Roberts, Llandaff) enters with St Teilo (Reverend R.S. Crockett, Grangetown), St Kentigern and St Beuno, and on being asked by Ceredig to help in the sacrifice, he replies that they

THE VICAR OF ABERPERGWM AS 'DEWI SANT'

cannot, as they are Christians. An incredulous Ceredig expostulates: 'Christians in Cymru! Never! Is there then a Cymric Church?' To which Teilo replies: 'Blessed be God, there is.' And Ceredig orders his warriors to 'leave those Christians to their rites'.[40]

What with princes (Mr Dudley Stuart, Dinas Powys, was 'Prince Dunod'), splendidly attired princesses (Mrs Dudley Stuart was 'Princess Bronwen' and Miss Williams, St Donat's Castle, was 'Princess Eurfron'), chiefs, warriors, priests, Christians – both free and captive – the scene certainly made an impact as visual spectacle, and the shrieking human sacrifice froze the blood. Leading onto the third wave of 'Cymry' to reach Wales, settling in Glamorgan and Monmouthshire, the second scene showed St Dyfrig (Mr G. Morris, Colum Road) and St Cadoc (Reverend L. Evans, De Burgh Street) of the second wave, together with their kinsman, Dewi Sant (Reverend Llewelyn Thomas, vicar of Aberpergwm), meeting Beli the Great, Prince of the Scots (or Irish), together with other princes and converting them to Christianity.

They are persuaded by St Dyfrig (supported by St Cadoc), who reminds them that when King Arthur defeated their fathers he had a shield on which was emblazoned the Cross of Christ. Cadoc urges them: 'Bear ye the Cross upon your shields, and win as Arthur won.' In answer to Beli's question as to what they should do, his followers reply: 'Ay, let us win.' And in answer to Beli's plea, 'Give us the sign', Dewi takes the Christian shield and gives it to him, whereupon he promptly discards his own. To a general shout of 'Allelujah!', Dewi leads them away and the thousands seated in the grandstand arise as the mixed choir of 250 voices, the women costumed 'à la' Lady Llanover, begin to sing Handel's 'Hallelujah Chorus' with great fervour. With the adoption of the Cross, Rhoscomyl's warriors are empowered by a quintessentially Victorian muscular Christianity as they march onward in pursuit of an ever widening empire. Henceforth, the Cross is essentially their talisman and their licence to take what they covet.[41]

The third episode, circa 943 AD, which brings some 150 players on stage, caused much excitement: Alderman Lewis Morgan, the Lord Mayor of Cardiff, in the role of Hywel Dda, one of Rhodri Mawr's grandsons, comes with his retinue to arrest the 'Ruffians' led by the 'Chief Ruffian' in the person of Captain Lindsay, the Chief Constable of

A SECTION OF THE PAGEANT CHOIR

Glamorgan. They are about to bear away some of the fair maids of the Tywi Valley following a barbarous raid on their rural community. The *Book of the Words* explains how Hywel, son of Cadell, king of Deheubarth, set about revising and codifying the ancient laws which had fallen into disuse. In so doing, law and order was enforced by a king who was both warrior and enlightened legislator, and whose laws were to remain in force for seven hundred years in Wales. This episode was meant to dramatize the civilizing effect Hywel's reforms had on Welsh life in general, and would doubtless go down well in today's Cardiff in the event of a revival of the 1909 production. Rhoscomyl would have relished a confrontation with our nocturnal 'Ruffians' on St Mary Street!

As assorted villains, mounted and on foot, are terrorizing fair maids, traders and clerics, burning habitations and enslaving the inhabitants, Hywel Dda comes upon them with his household troops, his son and heir apparent, Owen (Councillor William Jones), and a party of princes. They are followed by the sage, Blegywryd, Archdeacon of Llandaff, and other wise counsellors who bring the law to bear on the miscreants as soon as they have been rounded up by mounted avengers and brought before Hywel Dda for judgement:

> Evil ones! Children of reft and slaughter! Your day is done. Laws have we made by which ye shall be judged. For the blood of every man whom ye have slain, and all the crimes that ye have committed, ye shall pay full tale – full weight to the uttermost farthing. I have spoken. I Hywel, King of the Cymry.[42]

On Hywel Dda's command, Blegywryd unrolls 'the skins of the Law' to show them to the people, who rejoice as the king declares: 'Behold the charter of Right and Justice, which shall endure in the land henceforth for ever.' As foretold at the beginning by the chorus as they sang *'Codiad yr Haul'*, the sun of goodness had truly risen on a more orderly Wales.

Lord Mayor Lewis Morgan as 'Hywel Dda'

THE ARREST OF THE 'RUFFIANS'

It was an episode effervescently recounted in *The Western Mail*'s 'Pageant Pictures' supplement, telling of 'rustic beauty . . . dissolved into terrified disorder'. Indeed, it claimed that: 'Salvador Rosa has never peopled an immortal canvas with outlaws so convincing as that wild mob of which Captain Lionel Lindsay . . . was the leader.' As Hywel Dda, the impressively costumed Lord Mayor of Cardiff 'spoke with a voice ringing so firm and clear that it could be heard in most parts of the stand, and he added to his bearing, without theatricality, the kingly gesture and conviction that we instinctively associate with Howel the Good'. Full of vigour, movement and colour, the whole scene in its realistic recreation of the past could be said to be 'perhaps the most comprehensive and in some ways the most effective episode in the Pageant'.[43]

Dr Ellis Paxon Oberholtzer, a leading American pageant-master who had staged a highly successful historical pageant in Philadelphia in 1908, was an excited spectator in Cardiff in 1909. Commenting on the Hywel Dda episode, one thing in particular had impressed him:

> How girls could be found to be slung over the saddlebows of your riders and taken off as captives with their hair streaming down the horses' flanks is a mystery to me. I should despair of being able to find them in America.[44]

Someone should have explained to him that the daughters of 'Dame Wales' were nothing if not tractable. It is true that there were suffragettes around, but they had gone in pursuit of David Lloyd George, MP, in the National Eisteddfod held at the Royal Albert Hall in London a month before. And we know what kind of welcome Rhoscomyl would have given them in Sophia Gardens.

'HYWEL DDA' ARRESTS THE 'CHIEF RUFFIAN'

Five scenes follow in the third interlude as the Pageant moves into the Norman period. The first, circa 1050, has Gruffydd ap Llywelyn (Mr Iestyn Williams, Westgate Chambers, Newport), another of Rhodri Mawr's grandsons and a ruthless, battle-hardened king, intent on consolidating his territorial gains before his death in 1063 by 'planting' Elystan Glodrydd and his kin in 'this fruitful land of Morgan', enjoining them 'to hold it and keep it true to us', which they swear to do. Accompanied by his queen, Edith of the Swan Neck (Miss Nest Williams, St Donat's Castle), daughter of Algar, the Earl of Mercia, they are an arresting pair, he in 'purple velvet robes' befitting his masterful

MISS NEST WILLIAMS AS
'EDITH OF THE SWAN NECK'

character, she in 'mauve robes, richly embroidered with gold, and gold crown, gorget, and wimple'.[45]

By the time of the second scene, introduced by the band playing 'Old French Hunting Music' by Demersmann, the Normans, circa 1092, are in Glamorgan, whose independence has been reasserted by Iestyn ap Gwrgan (Colonel Henry Lewis, Greenmeadows). Having quarrelled with Rhys ap Tudor, a cousin and namesake of Rhys ap Tudor, king of Deheubarth, Iestyn promised his daughter, Nest (Mrs Henry Lewis, Green-meadows), in marriage to Einion ap Cadivor (Mr Henry Lewis, Green-meadows) on condition that Einion brought in with him his own tribe and a force of Normans. Thus supported he kills Rhys ap Tudor, pays off the Normans, but refuses Einion his share of the bargain – Nest as his wife. Einion promptly recalls the Normans led by Robert Fitzhamon, goes in pursuit of Iestyn, captures him and takes the willing Nest for his bride.[46]

Iestyn and Nest are returning from the hunt when Einion comes to claim her, so that there are horses aplenty as well as the famous Greenmeadow pack of hounds to make this an action-packed scene from the outset. With the return of the furiously galloping Normans and the ensuing fight with Iestyn's band, the onlookers were left breathless:

> There is no mere acting. It is a real wild chase conducted by experienced horsemen. The precipitous, headlong gallop, the foaming horses pushing each other and rearing in the rush, the

glittering armour and the gay garments of the warriors, the sombre castle of Cardiff in the background and the pack of hounds, nosing for a scent. It is a spectacle which grows upon the crowd every moment until a huge cheer breaks forth from the assembled multitude as Iestyn is hemmed in and captured.[47]

Dr Oberholtzer, yet again, could only marvel at the Greenmeadow pack of hounds, which he described as 'the best behaved animals I have ever seen on a field'. The 'Dame Wales' country was doing itself proud.

Without a word being said, the third scene presents Nest, the daughter of Rhys ap Tudor, king of Deheubarth, who 'no less than Helen of Troy, Cleopatra, and Mary Queen of Scots, was the cause of endless trouble among her admirers'. With the band playing Sant

THE LEWISES OF GREENMEADOW

Saens's 'Softly Awakes My Heart' with solo cornet, Nest (the eye-catching Mrs Charles Forester-Walker, Pengam) enters with her ladies, followed in succession by the men in her life – Gerald of Windsor, Owen ap Cadogan, Henry I 'who came to Wales for her sake' and, finally, Stephen, the Norman castellan of Cardigan Castle. The success of this scene centred on the impression made by Nest, and Mrs Forester-Walker was equal to the challenge:

> ... in an exquisite shade of shimmering satin, gold embroidered. A crown, from which hangs many chains of pearls, is poised on her beautifully coiffed hair. The Court robe is bordered with ermine. One cannot but be grateful for the pleasure given to the eye by this robe and its satin underdress.[48]

Yes, Nest was a resplendent beauty, but Rhoscomyl had to note in the *Book of the Words* that it was a beauty that also bred triumphant warriors, her sons, grandsons and great-grandsons leading the way in the conquest of Ireland, while Einion, her son by Owen ap Cadogan, 'was ancestor in the male line to Oliver Cromwell, the next conqueror of Ireland'. To quote Rhoscomyl: 'It seemed, in truth, as if no man could be descended from her without being a gallant fighter.'[49]

The fourth and fifth scenes also dispense with dialogue, it being left to the band and the chorus to evoke the proper mood. As the notes of Gounod's 'Andante Maestoso' subside at the beginning of the fourth scene, Robert Consul (Mr Treharne, Coed-ar-hyd-y-glyn), Earl of Gloucester and Prince of Glamorgan, a renowned patron of learning, emerges from the Castle with his court, which includes his half-sister, Maud, Queen of England (Mrs Hillier, Ninian Road, Cardiff). He is to meet with the three 'greatest scholars of Christendom at that time' – Geoffrey of Monmouth, Walter Map and Gerald the Welshman – to be presented with their 'immortal works': Geoffrey's *Historia Regum Britanniae*, Walter's reputed 'High History of the Holy Grail' (another Rhoscomyl discovery) and Gerald's *Itinerarium Kambriae*. Admitting to a 'slight inaccuracy' in that Robert Consul had died before Gerald the Welshman was born, Rhoscomyl felt justified in bringing the three 'illuminati' before the illustrious patron in order to highlight a brilliant cultural achievement of Norman Wales. And the Queen of England's presence certainly added to the splendour of the occasion as she appeared 'in full court robes of blue, blue velvet corsage thickly studded with pearls, gold jewelled crown, and veil. Her elaborate train [was] . . . carried by three smart pages in plum-coloured velvet tunics, blue hose, and blue caps'.[50]

The fifth scene commemorates Gwenllian (Mrs Delme Davies-Evans, Penylan, Golden Grove), the wife of Gruffydd ap Rhys, king of Deheubarth, sister of Owen Gwynedd and mother of the renowned Lord Rhys (1132-97). A warrior-woman of Rhoscomyl spirit, as his chapter on her in *Flame-Bearers of Welsh History* testifies, in 1136 she gathered her forces in her husband's absence and sent them to oppose a Norman army. With a small company she stayed behind to stop the garrison at Kidwelly Castle from breaking out to attack her larger force in the rear, but treachery conspired to catch her between two fronts. Her force was slaughtered, her two younger sons killed and she, also, taken prisoner and beheaded. She was avenged at the battle of Cardigan by the men of Deheubarth and Gwynedd, and as the choir sings 'Dewch i'r Frwydyr' (Into Battle), Gwenllian, her slain sons and a small party of warriors march past in battle array, Gwenllian 'in white, with cuirass of gold scale armour' followed by representatives of her avengers.[51]

The choir of 'Rhyvelgyrch Cadpen Morgan' introduces the fourth episode, generally regarded as the most exhilarating of the Pageant's five episodes. The cast numbered several hundred, as many as 500 said to be rugby players recruited by Mr W.T. Morgan, the president of Cardiff RFC, to serve as Ivor Bach's warriors in his assault on Cardiff Castle, circa 1158. Burdened by taxes imposed on them by the barons, who in turn had to pay tribute to Earl William of Gloucester (Mr W. Staniforth, Landsdowne Road School), the men of Glamorgan revolt and the barons flee to the castle for the Earl's protection.

MISS LUIE AS 'QUEEN GWENLLIAN'
(UNDERSTUDY FOR MRS DELME DAVIES-EVANS)

ROTARY PHOTO. E.C.   "THE NATIONAL PAGEANT OF WALES."
EPISODE IV.

THE RIGHT HON. LADY MAYORESS OF CARDIFF, MRS. LEWIS MORGAN
"PRINCESS HAWYS."

MR R. LEWIS JUNIOR,
GREENMEADOW AS 'IVOR BACH'

Insisting on treating with him and no other, the 'rebels' are confronted by an enraged William who threatens them with instant death on the morrow if they do not meet the barons' demands. They are adamant that they will only pay the dues as set by 'the old laws of the Cymry'. They remind him that they are free men and on his return to the castle they send a man on horseback to alert Ivor Bach – Ivor ap Cadivor, Lord of Senghennydd (Mr R. Lewis, Junior, Greenmeadow, one of his descendants). As the band plays 'Ar Hyd y Nos' (All Through the Night), he comes with armed men to lead an attack on the Norman's stronghold. Desperately trying to repel a frontal assault, William's men neglect the eastern wall, which is quickly scaled. The garrison is over-powered and Earl William and his family are taken prisoner and not released until he, of his own free will, has signed the Treaty of Senghennydd and agreed that:

> So long as sun and sea endure, the Men of the Bro shall pay no more of dues than their fathers paid before them in the days of old.

Once the Earl had signed, Ivor Bach, for his part, commits the 'Men of the Bro' to be 'true and faithful to the Lords of Cardiff . . . so long as this treaty is kept'. Quite simply, they were not revolutionaries (certainly not of Chartist stock); they were simply proponents of fair play. (What, one wonders, was Rhoscomyl's view of the Rhondda's striking miners in 1910?) Earl William and his people return to Cardiff Castle and Ivor

Bach with his men marches off to the stirring tune of 'Rhyvelgyrch Gwŷr Morgannwg' (The War Song of the Men of Glamorgan).[52]

There is no mistaking the point Rhoscomyl is making. As Caradoc and the Silures in the first episode unhesitatingly confronted the might of Rome, so Ivor Bach and his warriors in defence of Welsh rights do not hesitate to attack the Norman oppressor in his castle. And by dint of superior leadership and valour aplenty, they triumph – they scale the walls, they reject tyranny, they do not slaughter their prisoners but on the contrary negotiate a just settlement of their grievances before reaffirming their acceptance of their position in relation to their Norman overlords. It is as if the military and moral strengths of Caradoc and Hywel Dda have come together in Ivor Bach to effect a fine victory for common justice and civilized conduct in war, putting to shame the Norman 'chivalry' that butchered Gwenllian in Kidwelly. Lord Aberdare (William Napier Bruce, 1858-1936), after toying with the idea, must have regretted not playing Rhoscomyl's Ivor Bach 'in his full suit of chain

THE CASTLE IS TAKEN

armour, helm, and gorget, complete tunic lined with gold and trimmed silver'. But he didn't see himself as the obvious choice for the part:

> Should you wish me to appear in the part of my ancestor, Ivor Bach, coming down from the hills to sack the town I will think of it – but both Lord Bute and Lord Plymouth are nearer to the direct Lewis descent, and should be applied to first.[53]

What a pity that the three of them didn't agree to play him in turn.

It is obvious from *The Western Mail*'s description of the fourth episode that it impacted on the spectators like a relieving cavalry charge in an early 'Cowboys and Indians' film. It released a great charge of excitement:

> The details in the carrying out of the episode surpassed anything that could have been imagined . . . Norman barons, mounted on spirited horses, and wearing bright silver armour that flashes in the sun; stately ladies, attired in robes of the exquisite colours and designs of the period, re-endow with its medieval glories the Castle where the Prince of Glamorgan held Court and whence he ruled with tyrannous hand the surrounding clansmen. There was all the pomp and glory of baronial splendour about the surroundings; all the lofty Norman contempt for a conquered race about the treatment of the clansmen. The thing had gone beyond endurance . . . Across the field, close on the heels of Ivor Bach's galloping steed, rushed his gallant men, making for the Castle. Their clothes of white and purple fluttered gaily in the breeze. Pike and glaive flashed brightly as they sped . . . From the east and from the front armed men pressed on the Castle and scaled its walls. The Norman knights in armour tried in vain to stop the rush. It was wild and irresistible. It was made with all the elan of real battle . . . The whole episode from beginning to end was of a most dramatic and thrilling kind, and it is one which no other Pageant is likely to equal.[54]

NATIONAL PAGEANT OF WALES

CARDIFF JULY 26 TO AUG. 7. 1909.

FOOTBALLERS' FEROCIOUS ONSLAUGHT.

IVOR BACH STORMING CARDIFF CASTLE.

The account in *The South Wales Daily News* was similarly elated:

> The spectators will long remember how the blood was sent coursing through their veins by the stirring scenes, and all the scores of men who helped in Episode IV will be able to look back upon their work with pardonable pride, for it was good – decidedly good.[55]

Rhoscomyl had seized the opportunity to illustrate the military prowess of the Welsh in truly spectacular fashion, as Ivor Bach and his warriors accomplished a feat 'unequalled by any concerted deed of valour done by the Normans in the brilliancy of its conception and in the daring impetuosity of its execution'. No Rimington Scout could have bettered Ivor Bach's deed nor denied him the right to sport the leopard's claw.

Llywelyn Fawr (Mr Morgan Williams, St Donat's Castle) dominates the first scene in the fourth interlude. Set in Beaupre in Glamorgan, circa 1215, this scene shows him securing his position and his rights as

Prince of Wales in negotiations with the Lords Marcher, led by Gilbert Clare, Lord of Glamorgan, over the final version of Magna Charta. On receiving the scroll of the Charter from the Bishop of Llandaff (Reverend E.P. Jones, Llanbleddian Gardens), he shows it to the Lords, who express their satisfaction and, to cheers of 'Cymru am byth' and 'Clare!', they depart. Of particular interest in this scene was the authenticating presence of Mr Philip Basset, Llanbleddian, as a direct descendant of Basset of Beaupre, his wife also appearing as Dame Basset, while Mr A.W. Swash, the Pageant's impeccable secretary, together with his wife, took the parts of Ednyfed ap Cynric and his spouse, Angharad. The Pageant makes clear that Llywelyn Fawr has

MR PHILIP BASSET AS 'BASSET OF BEAUPRE'

come to treat from a position of strength as an equal, cutting an impressive figure wearing 'a most handsome embroidered white tabard over his chain armour', and the importance of the event enacted also seems reflected in the gorgeous costumes of the assembled ladies: Dame Basset, for example, appeared 'in grey robe, bodice embroidered and jewelled, and blue satin mantle, embroidered gold fleur-de-lys, and lined with pink silk'.[56]

Then comes tragedy as in the second scene 'Llywelyn Olav', killed on 11 December 1282, leads on the eighteen warriors who fell on Pont Orewyn fighting to the end. Undone by treachery, Llywelyn and his squire, running without armour to join the war band posted on the bridge over the Irfon, were met and run through by charging horsemen. Not a word is uttered during this scene, Llywelyn (Mr Isaac Vaughan Evans) leading them 'in solemn procession', a splash of blood

MR ISAAC VAUGHAN EVANS AS 'LLYWELYN OLAV'

on each warrior's forehead 'in token of his gallant death'. Bearing in mind the abject failure of the project – first noted in the 1850s and abandoned some sixty futile years later – to erect a national memorial for him, silence, apart from the choir's singing of 'Dafydd y Garreg Wen' (David of the White Rock), best became this scene – but it was, of course, a most reverent silence. A contributor in *The Nationalist* found refuge in bathos: 'My blood tingled at the sight, and in looking around me I noticed fair women weeping and strong men white with excitement. And at that moment we were all so proud of our nationality.' It is a relief to find in *The Western Mail* a somewhat more measured comment: 'It is a commemorative tableau, sad in the extreme, and unaided by any extraneous details, the march of the last Welsh Prince and his men is a striking silhouette which always comes in for the applause of the public.'[57]

The spectators could not be left contemplating death, or even worse, guilt, and the mood is changed to one of delight in the third scene, circa 1330, as the famed love-poet of medieval Wales, Dafydd ap Gwilym, dances with twenty-five of his desired beauties – represented by 'the most beautiful women among the school teachers of Cardiff'. Perhaps, ruminated one commentator, some of his poems might be thought 'rather too rich to be considered quite delicate from a modern point of view', but the dance was in the best taste as the beauties, in 'pale heliotrope gowns', joined with Dafydd in 'a "pas de vingt-et-un" which is most alluring to gaze upon'. *The Times* correspondent, obviously not familiar with Dafydd's poetic persona, commented favourably on his modesty: 'They dance delightfully; then group themselves adoringly round him, and when he has postured poet-wise a little, he flees man-wise from their embarrassing affection.'[58] But not for long!

Then, to the stirring music of Handel's 'March in Scipio', the fourth scene celebrates the proclamation of Owen Glyndwr as Prince of Wales at the old fortress of Caer Drewyn, near Corwen, on 20 September 1400. On Glyndwr entering with his family and three standard-bearers, the bards gather about him and present him to the

DAFYDD AP GWILYM DANCES WITH HIS 'CONQUESTS'

people as *'Mab y Darogan'* (the 'Heir of the Prophecies'). They respond with a great shout of acclamation. Having overthrown false Lord Grey of Rhuthin and started a war of liberation, he is come to issue a call to arms. He commands the standard-bearers first to shake out the Prince's banner bearing the arms of Llywelyn Fawr, four lions rampant, and secondly to shake out 'the banner of Wales, the old war flag of the Cymry' – a Red Dragon rampant on a white ground. A huge roar of approval goes up, and with the words 'Duw vo'n llwydd! God be our leader!', Glyndwr leads off.[59]

What made the scene resonate with the applauding thousands was the appearance of Godfrey Charles Morgan, Lord Tredegar (1831-1913), in the role of Glyndwr, dressed in dark blue and crimson, with Lady Llangattock as his wife resplendent in 'a magnificent robe of green velvet, embroidered with gold, over which [she wore] a crimson velvet mantle richly embroidered with gold, head-dress of crimson velvet and gold, veil of gold tissue'. They were accompanied by lineal descendants of historical figures who had featured in Glyndwr's life. Sir John Scudamore, who married Glyndwr's daughter, Alice, was represented by Mr Edward Courtenay Scudamore of Rhymney, and Alice by Mrs Colonel E.S.L. Scudamore, Kentchurch Court, Herefordshire. Jenkin Hanmer, Glyndwr's brother-in-law, was represented by Sir Wyndham Hanmer,

Lord Tredegar as 'Owen Glyndwr'

Bellisfield, Salop, and Margaret, another of Glyndwr's daughters, was played by Miss Margaret Hanmer. The presence of Miss Vaughan, Rheola, Neath, as 'Isabel Scudamore', dressed in white 'with overdresses of an exquisite shade of blue', also added to the glitter of the procession. It was a scene that exuded nobility, with Lord Tredegar, a living embodiment of the unquestioning heroism that Tennyson immortalized in 'The Charge of the Light Brigade', giving Glyndwr as Wales's evergreen historic and folkloric freedom fighter a further boost in public esteem.[60]

A scion of a splendid old Welsh family famed for its patronage of Welsh culture, Lord Tredegar's participation in the Pageant must have pleased Rhoscomyl no end. Here was a cultivated, fearless Welsh warrior, and a horseman to boot who, to the glory of the British Empire, as one of the 'gallant six hundred' had charged the Russian guns on 25 October 1854 on the heights above Balaclava. Next to having ridden alongside him in that mad Crimean caper, Rhoscomyl could not have wished for more than his patrician support for 'the great venture' in Sophia Gardens – a charge this time to popularize Welsh history that would surely not be branded a folly. *The Western Mail* had no doubts about the value of Lord Tredegar's participation. 'His scene' was in all respects a signal triumph:

> His [Glyndwr's] representative at the Pageant is one of the most loved Welshmen of our day, a man who in culture and courage comes close to the ideal conception of Glyndwr. When it was seen that Viscount Tredegar was acting the part of Glyndwr and Lady Llangattock the part of his wife, the demonstration in the stand was, perhaps, as remarkable a tribute as has been paid to a popular nobleman. The spectators rose to their feet enthusiastically cheering, cheering the personality no less than the singular beauty of the scene in which he was the central and commanding figure. It was a short, but a very thrilling, scene, and the spectators cheered again and again when the Standard-

LADY LLANGATTOCK AS 'GLYNDWR'S' WIFE

MISS PEREGRIN AS ELIZABETH
'DAUGHTER OF OWEN GLYNDWR'

bearer, at the bidding of Glyndwr, shook out the banner of the Prince of Wales and then the old war flag of the Cymry. Not for long will one forget the gay cavalcade of colour, the mail-clad knights, and the beautiful robes of the ladies, and over all the banners of Wales floating triumphantly in the breezes, as Owen Glyndwr led the way to the exit.[61]

As for the cheering crowds, it is more than likely that they saw Glyndwr standing tall in Lord Tredegar's reflected glory, rather than their favourite Lord growing in stature thanks to Glyndwr's legendary fame. But they were happy to salute both as brothers in arms.

The fifth and final episode and interlude move quickly to Rhoscomyl's purposeful conclusion. The Pageant would demonstrate how Wales begat the Tudor dynasty, from which sprang the Anglo-Celtic empire that was still a formidable world power in 1909. If Glyndwr's war of liberation had failed in the fifteenth century, he had nevertheless found sanctuary 'in the heart of every true Cymro', where 'from generation to generation' his spirit would be 'dreaming on, dreaming on, safe for ever and for ever'. And who better to show that spirit still at work than Shakespeare, the voice of England, who in *Henry IV, part 2* commends Glyndwr's worthiness. The fifth episode, based on acts four and five of *Henry V*, follows the Welsh warriors to the battlefield of Agincourt where the archers secure a famous victory, where 'Fluellen', a Welsh captain, reminds the king that 'All the water in Wye cannot wash your majesty's Welsh plood out of your body', and then cudgels Pistol into eating the leek he had mocked on St David's Day.[62]

'Fluellen' (i.e. Llywelyn), played by Ernest Cove 'in gold-studded cuirass and green cap with feathers', embodies a Rhoscomyl warrior's respect for 'the law of arms', a readiness to defend the honour of his native land and a steadfast loyalty to his king who, in return, is proud to own to his Welsh descent. It is as if Rhoscomyl already had in mind the Investiture of the Prince of Wales in 1911 and was using 'Fluellen' to signal to his countrymen the conduct that would befit them on that occasion. They would be in the presence of royalty, and in the Pageant's King Henry V (Mr Victor Wiltshire) they had a foretaste of majesty as he stood before them 'in a complete suit of brass armour and visor, crimson plush robe, and ermine cape'.

In a bustling, kaleidoscopic scene that brings on all the relevant characters in Shakespeare's play, plus scores of soldiers, camp followers, French fugitives, French horsemen, monks, peasants and

Mr Victor Wiltshire as 'Henry V'

general stragglers, the opening chorus of *'Ymadawiad y Brenin'* (The King's Departure), with its refrain –

> Follow me, follow me
> Let our war cry be –
> Britain ever shall be free;
> We will die for liberty.

– immediately strikes the right note with the spectators. It is hardly likely that they would have heard much of Shakespeare's dialogue, but they would have been compensated for that by 'a scale of splendour' that was exceptional at a time when 'pageantism' was so popular.[63]

The first scene in the concluding interlude has Owen Tudor (Mr Godfrey Williams, Aberpergwm) who had fought alongside Henry V at Agincourt, dancing at the Court of his widowed Queen, Catherine (Mrs Godfrey Williams), at Baynard's Castle, where he is one of her bodyguards. As they dance a pavane – the band playing Gabriel Mari's 'La Cinquantaine' – Owen trips over his feet and stumbles against the amused Catherine. That most fortuitous stumble begins a love affair that became a marriage and it was Edmund, one of their two sons, who fathered Henry VII, the first monarch of the Tudor dynasty. A Welsh warrior who had fought at Agincourt and became a widowed Queen's darling, was to be found at the source of what would be for a tumultuous period in British history the world's greatest imperial mission. It needed a dazzling scene to do justice to such a providential liaison and *The Western Mail* was inclined to give it pride of place in its review of the Pageant:

> Queen Katherine is the Hon. Mrs Godfrey Williams. The character is here presented in an ideal manner. Mrs Williams looks bewitching in her robe of grey satin, gold surcoat, blue mantle richly embroidered with fleur-de-lys, with a soft bordering of ermine, pure and creamy, against the rich velvet. Owen Tudor . . .

the gay and graceful favourite of the Queen, is in gold embroidered white satin and black velvet cap.[64]

All the glittering, dancing courtiers seem to presage the coming age of splendour.

The second scene takes place in a field near the church of Stoke Golding as the battle of Bosworth, 1485, comes to a bloody end to the sound of the band playing Volkmann's 'Tragic overture to Richard III'. Henry, Earl of Richmond, Owen Tudor's grandson, enters with his principal supporters, including Jasper Tudor, the Earl of Pembroke, the Earl of Oxford, Lord Stanley, Sir William Stanley, Rhys ap Thomas, Sir John Savage, Reginald Bray and of course Richard ap Howel of Mostyn, played by his direct lineal descendant, Lord Mostyn. A crowd of clamorous soldiers follows them, one of whom has found the slain Richard III's crown. It is taken by Lord Stanley and placed on Henry Tudor's head, whereupon a wild shout goes up from one and all. Then, in recognition of Richard ap Howel's total commitment to his cause, Henry Tudor urges him to come to Court 'where thou shalt be advanced beyond thy dreams', only to receive a famous reply: 'I dwell amongst mine own people.' Henry then unbuckles his sword and gives it to Richard ap Howel with the words: 'Then take thou this for token of all I owe to thee.' It is a

MR AND MRS GODFREY WILLIAMS AS 'OWEN TUDOR' AND 'CATHERINE'

short but highly charged scene, the few heartfelt words spoken serving to highlight that it was Welsh fidelity that secured the crown for Henry, fidelity rooted in a patriotism that sought no reward other than its own vindication.[65]

The third and final scene transports us to Ludlow where the Court and Council of Wales and the Marches had been long accustomed to deliberate. Amid much merrymaking on the Green, Bishop Rowland Lee, Lord President of the Council, comes from the Castle ahead of Sir John Price of Brecon and his followers with the intention of petitioning King Henry VIII when he arrives with his newly-wed Queen, Jane Seymour, and a numerous retinue including Lady St David's as 'The Lady of Dyved'. On arriving, Sir John Price presents him with a petition in the name of the Welsh people requesting the union of Wales with England. The King replies with the only words spoken at this re-enactment of a defining moment in the history of Wales:

LORD MOSTYN AS 'RICHARD AP HOWEL MOSTYN'

> My kin and faithful liegemen, I have hearkened to your prayer and granted your petition. Here is the Act of Union between England and Wales for ever.

And to the pealing of bells and loud shouts of joy Henry leads off, 'the assembled people fall into the rear and leave the scene amidst every manifestation of happiness and gratification'.[66]

A SECTION OF THE CAST ASSEMBLED
FOR THE 'FINALE'

The Pageant absolves Henry VIII of responsibilty for the Act that took an axe to the Welsh language and culture with results meant to be as deadly as the beheading of poor Anne Boleyn. One would like to think that this was Rhoscomyl's cryptic way of saying that in view of their ingrained subservience to England the Welsh had got not what they asked for as much as prayed for – but that would be much too fanciful. Not for nothing did the choir sing *'Breuddwyd y Frenhines'*, in which 'happy dream' the Queen sees 'Deadly foes in friendship blended':

> May her dream be no illusion,
> Only born to fade away;
> Ne'er again may wild confusion
> O'er her native land have sway.
> Banished far be care and sadness
> From her children brave and free;
> Blest abode of joy and gladness,
> May the fair isle ever be.[67]

It only remained to construct a finale that would live long in the memory, and it was generally agreed that in meeting the challenge G.P. Hawtrey excelled himself as pageant-master. For E.A. Morphy it was 'the most magnificent spectacle of any kind attempted in modern pageantry', in which 'a glowing mass' of some 5,000 players came together 'as in some gigantic ballet scene' on the Pageant field. It moved *The Western Mail* to rhapsodize:

> Here were the comings and the goings of the generations of Wales, peopling a canvas filled with a loftier romance and a fuller atmosphere than was ever painted even by a Turner. It was all 'a hallow'd memory like the names of old,' and about it floated eddies of melodious airs that carried us back to the Wales of the fighting men and the Wales of the mourners, and,

anon, to the Wales of rural peace. The procession left on one's mind the impression of a nation rich in colour and poetry, renowned in arms, famous in romance.[68]

When all the pageanteers were ranged in front of the grandstand 'Dame Wales', attended by the Counties, emerged again from the Castle. Again the fairies flocked to their respective Counties 'and groups spun out in lines forming a map of Wales in many colours'. Then everybody kneeled, 'and "Hen Wlad Fy Nhadau" rose from the vast throng – a thrilling and a splendid close'. It was left to the band to play 'God Save the King' as the pageanteers, grouped according to the episodes and interlude scenes they had enacted, withdrew, the fairies the last to dance away.[69]

The Western Mail had no doubts about the 'truth' of the Pageant's depiction of the Welsh past. It was equally convinced of the Pageant's validity as a medium for distilling history's romance and projecting its lessons:

> If it be the duty of history to make the past present, then the Pageant is history of the richest and most perfect kind, since it peoples the land anew with its ancient heroes and re-animates the scenes in which they lived and won their fame.

It simply remained for G.P. Hawtrey to receive the plaudits of fellow pageant-master Edward Baring, who had achieved a great success in Bath. In his opinion it was worth a journey to Cardiff if only to see the 'Finale', but he had found the entire performance inspiring: 'It is simply magnificent.' And he was far from being alone in thinking so. It was *The Daily Dispatch* that said of the closing scene:

> For a gargantuan feast of colour and beauty this excels anything ever attempted in pageantry ... The scene was altogether brilliant and impressive. The whole Pageant indeed, represents much of the wonder, the beauty, and the majesty of the great past of Wales.[70]

'The Fairies'
GATHER FOR THE LAST TIME

Owen Rhoscomyl's grave in the old cemetery at Rhyl

REVIEW

T FELL TO Cardiff's premier newspapers, *The Western Mail* and *The South Wales Daily News*, to hail the unprecedented success of The National Pageant of Wales. They had regularly forecast a triumph since the idea was first mooted and they were not about to limit themselves to modest congratulation when a fortnight's uninhibited 'padgeing' came to an end. After the very first day of the extraordinary event, the commentators made free with 'Cymric' excess:

> To young and old alike the Pageant reveals what no historian can – the life and the manners of other days and the events that have shaped the destinies of a great people . . . Here is an object lesson in the patriotism of other days . . . Here is set forth the highest art. Eye and ear are fascinated; the blood is stirred; the pulse beats. Never before has such a pageant been attempted, – never again, it may be, will such a pageant be presented.[1]

It was inconceivable that any Welsh person could experience such a celebration of heritage without a feeling of pride awakening in him or her 'a realization of what they had never fully appreciated before'.

The Western Mail[2] unhesitatingly declared that the Pageant was 'an absolutely unique event in the long and stirring and glorious history of Wales.' No longer would the Welsh patriot have to fear being seen as a crank after 'the brave show' made by 'gallant little Wales'. And it was 'not merely a delightful event: it was an education, an education in art, in colour, in harmony, in histrionics, and, above all, in history'. Between them, Rhoscomyl and G.P. Hawtrey had excelled Herodotus in brilliantly evoking the past, creating 'a living picture of Wales which has never yet been approached for truth and magnificence, and which is not likely to be approached again'.[3] Quoting an 'eminent critic' who held that 'the education, mental and physical, the increased vitality, the trained patriotism, that it brought into South Wales are inestimable', *The South Wales Daily News* felt no need to trim its judgement: 'Wales has shown the nations what a National Pageant can be; the triumph has been unparalleled in an age of popular pageantry.'[4]

No less assertive for being daily overshadowed by its two big sister papers was *The Cardiff Times and South Wales Weekly News*.[5] In its view the Pageant not only recreated history, it made history 'in firing the imagination of the people with a love of the pomp and the glitter and the old-time jollity of life in the field'. The whole purpose of pageantry was to activate the imagination so that a living engagement with the past became possible, and the sooner children hemmed in by mean streets experienced its liberating force so much the better, in all senses, for the health of their communities. Louis Napoleon Parker could have written these words:

> It is difficult to realise what this has meant to thousands of children confined to drab city streets, hundreds of whom have a grey outlook upon life, and if the Pageant leads the public to favour a return to country dances and dress pageants for the children, the gain will be great. As a set-off to the age of commercialism and competition, pageantry promises great things.[6]

The congratulations of sundry onlookers, particularly from beyond Wales, whose opinions were considered worth quoting were gratefully gathered. The Scottish MP James Murray, the American pageant-master Dr Ellis Paxon Oberholtzer, Edward Baring (the English pageant-master who had scored notable successes at the Cheltenham and Bath Pageants), the actor-manager F.R. Benson, and G.P. Hawtrey's brother, John, who adjudged the National Pageant at Cardiff the best he had seen – all their views were seized upon and reported with relish.[7] It was no small thing that the prestigious illustrated weekly, *The Sphere*,[8] had seen fit to make The National Pageant of Wales the subject of one of its distinctive supplements similarly, *The Times*,[9] despite noting that the crowd on the opening day was disappointing and noticeably short of working-class people, nevertheless wrote encouragingly about the undertaking, saying of the Ivor Bach episode that 'it goes with a roar, and is, indeed, one of the most stirring that modern pageantry has produced'.

In the absence of a royal personage to approve of the public celebration of something as abstruse (even suspect in some high circles) as Welsh history, the presence of the Lord Mayor and the Lady Mayoress of London on Saturday, 31 July, was hailed in Cardiff as a signal honour for Wales. Sir George Wyatt Truscott, in the civic dinner held in his honour in the City Hall, declared himself a proud Cornishman whose family motto *'Y Gwir yn erbyn y Byd'* (The Truth against the World) – was inspired by Iolo Morganwg. Recounting 'the stirring events of other days that shaped the destinies of a progressive and freedom-loving people', Sir George went on to insist that 'if there was one nation more than another which could be portrayed in pageantry, it was Wales, whose history was full of romance and charm'. With the Mayors and Mayoresses of Bath and Wandsworth in full agreement, Sir George gave voice to 'a paean of unqualified praise', emphasizing the importance of extolling the heroes of bygone days and, as reported in *The South Wales Daily News*, insisting that 'no son or daughter of Wales – or any Britisher for that matter – can afford to neglect the opportunity now provided for a visit to the finest theatre in the world', where they would witness 'the greatest of historical object-lessons yet presented'. As he subsequently told the Lord Mayor of Cardiff in a letter of appreciation, he had found the Pageant 'very imposing and realistic'.[10]

As the Pageant fortnight ended the Cardiff press spoke of a city momentarily released from the relentless pressures of trade, its people meandering through a haze of other days, other days cleansed of squalor, their spell unbroken by too insistent a concentration on stubborn facts and necessities. The close of 'the great venture' had been enriched by 'a rare Italian sunset' and then: 'A light mist from the river stole among the trees and turned the gathering gloom and fleeting figures into a perfect fairyland.' It was a scene to excite a Tintoretto or a Raphael, claimed a contributor to *The Nationalist*, and to the artist, Christopher Williams, this emphasized the magical quality of the Pageant at night:

> You see a group of figures in a strong light, and beyond and around them is darkness – mystery. The evening performances impress me as being more in the minor key, and in this respect in harmony with our Welsh music and also with Welsh art generally, for was not the best work of our greatest artists, G.F. Watts and Burne Jones, also in the minor key?[11]

It would appear that The National Pageant of Wales had succeeded in casting a spell that, no matter how short-lived, had brought the past into an imaginative relationship with contemporary Wales in a way that no other use of history had done before. It seemed at the time to have created a general mood that made its spectators more receptive to the appeal of their country's past and encouraged them to look at themselves in a more rewarding way. The Pageant as an early exploratory exercise in the creation of an imagined national community in Wales could not be said to have been without promise.

In his 'Retrospect' for *The Nationalist*,[12] G.P. Hawtrey marvelled at his cast of 'born actors', whose uninhibited approach to drama was for him 'one of the most striking characteristics of the race'. Likewise, their singing to the invaluable accompaniment of Lieutenant G. Miller's band had played a major part in the Pageant's success, proving, for instance, Miller's insistence on performing Handel's 'Hallelujah Chorus' at the end of the second interlude to have been inspired. Between them, the band and the chorus had delivered a stream of mood music that had engendered and sustained a splendid rapport between the players and the spectators. Hawtrey admitted that he had been accused on occasions of behaving like an 'Autocratic Brute', but with a little tact his huge cast had by and large taken kindly to being drilled by an Englishman and had performed magnificently, 'their imaginations all aflame with pride and love for their country's history, proud of their Pageant and full of loyalty'.

Given that this was the first venture of its kind in Wales, Hawtrey was on secure ground in claiming that his players had put on 'such a display that has never been seen in this country before'. But in saying that it was a display to silence the mockers and detractors of Wales he stood tall, at that euphoric moment, on the high ground of national approval. But those who mock are not that easily silenced. Mockery has been a constant in human history since the dawn of our post-lapsarian state, and it loves to perch in places where it expects to elicit soulful remonstration. That Wales has been one such place for far too long is still true at the beginning of the twenty-first century. Be that as it may, to have an Eton-educated English pageant-master announce in 1909 that mockers and detractors had been put to flight by a National Pageant he had felt it 'a high privilege and a great responsibilty' to manage, would sound in many Welsh ears as confirmation of deliverance from ancient spite.[13]

But what of Rhoscomyl's response? The historian who set such store by the soundness of his research, who challenged the spectators and the readers of the *Book of the Words* to find fault with his facts, did not have his say in *The Nationalist* after the Pageant was over. But the editor, Sir Marchant Williams, had given him space in March 1909 to whip up interest, which he had done with characteristic brio. Significantly, after boasting that his script would be 'historically accurate to the smallest detail', what most concerned him was that the history staged should be worthy of 'reverence' – nothing less – for, 'where reverence enters in, the highest good alone can follow'.[14] While talk of 'reverence' could be said to indicate a sacerdotal involvement with Welsh history, it seems more apt in Rhoscomyl's case to describe it as heraldic, because he saw that history as an escutcheon, and as such he would expect his followers to safeguard its nobility. He wanted them to feel as honour-bound as he himself to revere it, to grapple it to their hearts, to permit no defilement of it. Rhoscomyl's espousal of Welsh history was that of a man who 'had his very soul in pageantry', and it was for J. Glyn Davies something to be wondered at:

> He conceived Welsh history as a pageant . . . all splendour. Ancient brutalities and treacheries had no place in such a pageant . . . The very name 'Cymru' was sacred to him; put up that symbol, and all the sordidness and meanness that one finds in Wales, as in all countries, faded clean out of his vision.[15]

Strange to relate in view of Davies's words, Rhoscomyl was not swept up in the euphoria that swirled around in the immediate aftermath of the Pageant. He does not appear to have been elated by what was achieved. The press did report his appreciation of the soldiers from Cardiff barracks who had played the parts of the 'Ruffians' in the Hywel Dda episode and behaved impeccably, singing 'Goodbye, Dolly Grey' as they returned, banner unfurled, along Cathedral Road. But that apart, Rhoscomyl was little quoted by journalists eager to eulogize, whereas Hawtrey's views were given prominence and his contribution to the Pageant's success, along with that of the vigorously effective secretary, A.W. Swash, loudly acclaimed. It is a letter he wrote to J. Glyn Davies, dated 4 September

1909, which reveals what Rhoscomyl's personal view of the Pageant was and what he thought of Hawtrey's role in particular when it transpired that 'the great venture', despite repeated forecasts of inevitable success, had been a financial failure.[16]

In the run-up to the Pageant, what comment there was in the Cardiff press about the financial side of so large an undertaking was optimistic – very optimistic. At the beginning of 1909 a Guarantee Fund of between £7,000 and £10,000 was predicted and a profit anticipated, earmarked for a number of unnamed charities, of some £6,000 to £10,000. By the end of the first week in February, the Guarantee Fund had reached a sum of £3,568 and G.P. Hawtrey felt sufficiently sure of success to advance £50 of his own money. One paper quoted a figure of £16,000 as the approximate cost of preparing for, and staging, 'the great venture' – it was, after all, to be The National Pageant of Wales and it would be held in the city of Cardiff. It had to be a triumph.[17]

Despite assurances during the Pageant fortnight that a full account of the financial outcome would soon be made public, the weeks went by without anything appearing in either *The Western Mail* or *The South Wales Daily News*. Had the Pageant made a profit, surely the sum would have been rubricated in celebration of the astuteness of the committee members who, it was claimed, represented 'the keenest business circles in the most-go-ahead city of Britain'. That a national undertaking, 'in many respects one of the most remarkable public enterprises that were ever embarked upon by a body of Welshmen', should fail to pay its way in Edwardian Cardiff was too dismal a prospect to dwell upon. It was *The Cardiff Times and South Wales Weekly News*, 14 August 1909, that first admitted the unpalatable truth that the Pageant had not paid its way. It had certainly been a worthwhile venture, but it was neverthless a financial failure. Not only had it not attracted a Wales-wide audience, the populous districts of south Wales had not been enthused to the extent so confidently forecast. Quite simply, the people had not come to be enthralled and enlightened by their history.[18]

Early in November both *The Western Mail* and *The South Wales Daily News* carried reports of a decision taken by the Pageant's executive committee to hold a special meeting of guarantors at the City Hall on 8 November. Faced with a deficit of £2,154-8-0 (reduced to £2,054 by 8 November) each guarantor was expected to pay eight shillings in the pound to meet the loss incurred, and Lord Mayor Lewis Morgan wanted all questions properly put and answered to everyone's satisfaction. He made no bones about his personal disappointment with the financial outcome, drawing particular attention to some reasons for the failure to make a profit.[19]

First and most bitter to accept was the lack of public support from around Cardiff and further afield in Wales. The people had not come in their tens of thousands as the Pageant's promoters had blithely foretold. There had been no need for a grandstand costing £3,750 to seat 7,500 spectators, and the borrowed football stands 'were never anything like full'. Despite the tireless efforts of legions of volunteers it had still been necessary to employ many helpers to get the costumes ready in time, and the money taken at the gate had not compensated for unexpected costs. The Lord Mayor had received a letter, signed 'Guarantor', claiming that some 300,000 had come through the gates – more than enough to clear all the costs – but in fact fewer than 200,000 had attended the Pageant and of those 90,000 had paid tenpence or less. First-class tickets cost only 10/6d compared with two guineas and a guinea respectively at the profit-making York and Bath Pageants, and of those 10/6d tickets a mere 778 had been sold in Cardiff. Indeed, had it not been for zealous Cardiffians who came five and six times, The National Pageant of Wales would have been a 'shocking failure financially'.

Foul weather during the first week had certainly kept people away. It rained, forcing the cancellation of performances on Tuesday 27 July, rain that 'fell in torrents during every morning of the first week, at the very time when people would be making up their minds whether they would go to Cardiff or not'. It was soon obvious that the man in the

THE RETURN OF THE PENITENT

(A Staniforth cartoon)

street, generally not caring overmuch for history and hardly acquainted with pageantry, was not about to rush through the rain to pay 10/6d, 7/6d, 5/- or 2/6d for a reserved seat, or even a shilling for the right to sit in a football stand and watch for three hours. For the second week the prices of admission were halved and 14,000 seats set aside for shilling ticket-holders. The crowds grew appreciably as the sun shone at last, prompting the promoters to add another three well-supported evening performances, 9-11 July, to the official fortnight. But the losses incurred during that first rain-sodden week could not be recouped.

Even the hordes of schoolchildren for whom the Pageant was to have been an exhilarating experience of history had, in Lord Mayor Lewis

Morgan's view, militated against success. He regretted their coming in their thousands to rehearsals which were 'no more than unfinished practices', for on returning to their homes in the outlying districts they made most unhelpful remarks, 'such as that Henry VII was crowned with a straw hat, etc., [giving] their parents and friends an entirely erroneous impression of the Pageant as it was really presented'. Damned schoolchildren, forever coming between educators and their ideals, and in this particular case between Welsh history and an audience!

For the meeting of guarantors on 8 November, the honorary treasurer, John Allcock, FSSA, prepared a Statement of Accounts audited and found correct by Charles E. Dovey, FCA. It showed that an income of £13,904-3-9 against an expenditure of £16,058-11-9 left a deficit of £2,154-8-0 which could be cleared, at eight shillings in the pound, from a Guarantee Fund amounting to £5,386. Every guarantor received a copy of the Statement in advance of 8 November, *The South Wales Daily News* publishing a synopsis of it on 6 November, and it has been my good fortune recently to receive from Mr Matthew Williams, the assiduous archivist at Cardiff Castle, a copy of the original Statement of Accounts which has proved most helpful. It came together with a 'pro forma' letter of appeal, dated 11 September 1909, from the Lord Mayor to 'Dear Sir' or 'My Lord' seeking assistance in clearing a deficit of over £1,500. As most of the guarantors were 'poor people', the Pageant's promoters hoped to benefit from the generosity of their wealthier supporters who were 'in sympathy with the movement and with Welsh aspirations'.[20]

Simply to note some of the details of expenditure contained in the Statement of Accounts is to gain a better appreciation of the huge effort that went into trying to ensure the success of the Pageant. For example, the sums of money (here in pounds only) spent on 'Dresses and Properties' amounted to £3,348: as much as £1,761 on materials; £75 on designing and cleaning costumes; £40, £119 and £5 on purchasing costumes from the Winchester Pageant, the Cheltenham Pageant and the Denbigh Pageant respectively; £830 on wages for the

Wardrobe Mistress, Seamstresses and Property men, etc; £166 on boots, and £350 on wigs.

A sum of £965 was spent on 'Music': £734 for the Band of the Royal Marines, £30 for the Band of the Glamorgan Imperial Yeomanry and £10 for the services of the Cardiff Harmonic Society at concerts. 'Scenery' cost £223, £177 of which was spent on erecting the castle. 'Hire of Horses and Forage' amounted to £307. Expenditure on the 'Stands' totalled £4,716: it cost £3,483 to erect the grandstand and another £960 for the football stands, barricading, latrines, payboxes etc. 'Electric Lighting' cost £967. 'Telephones', the all-important telephones, cost £82. A total of £1,291 was spent on 'Advertising', including £93 for the Lord Mayor of London's luncheon. It cost £385 to publish the *Book of the Words*, and another £94 to publish the *Child's Book of the Words* (also prepared by Rhoscomyl). For the 'Services of Police' a sum of £105 was spent.

On the income side the items that fix attention are the following. 'Admission to the Pageant Performances' grossed £10, 814. The letting of 'Photographic Rights', 'Bioscopic Rights' and 'Souvenir Publishing Rights' brought in £52, £21 and £10 respectively, while the 'Rights for Supply of Refreshments' brought in another £75. Sales of the *Book of the Words* and the *Child's Book of the Words* amounted to £417 and £116. Firework displays, concerts and two dances (distinctly fashionable affairs) organized by an energetic 'Entertainment Committee' brought in sums of £174, £34 and £52 (clear profit), while 'Advertising' in the *Book of the Words*, the *Child's Book of the Words,* the 'Music Book' and the 'Programmes' amounted to £338. The 'Sale of Costumes, Properties, etc.,' brought in £367 and it would be truly rewarding if some of the costumes bought by many of the 1909 pageanteers were to reappear in 2009 in Mr Matthew Williams's projected Pageant Exhibition in Cardiff Castle. There must still be attics to explore!

Of particular interest is the information the Statement of Accounts provides about the 'Sale of Tickets' – a total of 175,258, which breaks down as follows:

EXPENDITURE

	£ s. d.	£ s. d
Brought forward		4,314 2 6
SCENERY—		
Erection of Castle	177 0 0	
Salary of Scenic Artist	43 12 9	
Services of Architect	5 0 0	225 12 9
HIRE OF HORSES AND FORAGE—		
Horse Hire	171 10 0	
Fodder	49 9 5	
Wages of Grooms	27 8 11	
Stores, Ropes, &c.	12 8 9	
Carriage of Goods, &c.	6 4 0	
Insurance of Horses	33 0 0	
Shoeing	1 10 6	
Miscellaneous	6 7 6	307 19 1
STANDS—		
Erection of Grand Stand	3,483 0 0	
Architects' Fees	185 14 0	
Insurance	24 12 1	
Advertising	2 11 0	
Wages of Clerk of Works, Caretaker, &c.	54 3 6	
	3,750 0 7	
Erection of Football Stands, Barricading, Latrines, Payboxes, &c.	960 19 1	
Insurance	5 2 9	4,716 2 5
ELECTRIC LIGHTING—		
Contract for Installation	825 0 0	
Use for three extra days	80 0 0	
Extras on Contract	35 17 6	
Flare Lamps	26 14 0	967 11 6
Carried forward		£10,531 8 3

PAGES FROM THE TREASURER'S ACCOUNTS FOR THE NATIONAL PAGEANT OF WALES,
AND A LETTER FROM JOHN ALLCOCK TO ALL THE PAGEANT GUARANTORS
REQUESTING FINANCIAL ASSISTANCE

INCOME

		£ s. d.	£ s. d.	£ s. d.
Brought forward	...			11,244 17 0

MEMO.—

	£	s.	d.
Pageant Performances ...	10,814	3	3
Firework Displays ...	174	0	6
Concerts, etc. ...	34	5	3
	£11,022	9	0

Tickets sold by Railway Companies as follows:—

	TICKETS.	£ s. d.	£ s. d.
Taff Vale Railway			
Great Western Railway ...	8,782 @ 10d.	365 18 4	
Rhymney Railway ...	8,185 @ 10d.	341 0 10	
Barry Railway ...	2,328½ @ 10d.	97 0 5	
London & North Western Railway	1,723½ @ 10d.	71 16 3	
Brecon & M...		18 19 7	
		1 1 3	895 16 8
	...	75 0 0	
	...	52 10 0	
	...	21 0 0	
	...	10 0 0	158 10 0
		417 8 2	
		116 18 3	
		1 1 0	
		22 14 9	
			558 2 2
			12,857 5 10

CITY HALL,
CARDIFF,

5th November, 1909.

Dear Sir (or Madam),

WELSH NATIONAL PAGEANT.

I am instructed by the Executive Committee of the above Pageant to enclose a Statement of Accounts. I regret that there is a deficiency equal to 8/- in the £ on the amount guaranteed.

Your attendance is requested at a Meeting of the Guarantors which will be held in the Council Chamber, City Hall, Cardiff, on Monday next, the 8th inst., at 8 p.m.

You kindly guaranteed £ 5 : 0 : 0 , and I shall be glad if you will be so good as to send me within the next few days a remittance for £ 2 : 0 : 0 , being at the rate of 8/- in the £, in order that the outstanding liabilities may be discharged.

All cheques to be made payable to me and crossed National Provincial Bank of England, Ltd., Welsh National Pageant.

Yours faithfully,

JOHN ALLCOCK,
Hon. Treasurer.

Ed Thomas Esq.

Adults	Children
778 @ 10/6	37 @ 5/3
823 @ 7/6	48 @ 3/9
1,735 @ 5/-	450 @ 2/6
60 @ 4/-	2,429 @ 1/3
558 @ 3/-	
27,487 @ 2/6	School Children
2 @ 2/3	55,727 @ 3d
1,702 @ 2/-	
32 @ 1/6	
66,779 @ 1/	
13,178 @ 6d	

The agreement made with a number of railway companies, whereby a combined railway and admission ticket could be purchased from all stations within fifty miles of Cardiff (including Llanelli, Hereford and Gloucester) for a fare and a quarter, plus tenpence, accounted for 21,500 of all ticket sales:

8,782 on the Taff Vale Railway,
8,185 on the Great Western Railway,
2,328 on the Rhymney Railway,
1,723 on the Barry Railway,
455 on the London and North Western Railway,
25 on the Brecon and Merthyr Railway.

It was an arrangement that, in keeping with all the preparations for the Pageant, had been well thought out and could have been expected to be much better supported. As the members of the executive committee gathered to meet the guarantors at the City Hall, it was a feeling of being 'more sinned against than sinning' that united them. In the event, the explanations provided by Lord Mayor Lewis Morgan and treasurer John Allcock were well received by their audience – Lewis Morgan making a particular point of emphasizing that for the Lord Mayor of

London's civic reception he, as Lord Mayor of Cardiff, had borne most of the cost of preparing a fitting welcome and hospitality. After a formal vote of thanks to all the volunteers, 'the meeting, which was of a most amicable character, came to a close'. Indeed, it had been so amicable that the executive committee immediately reconvened to propose a vote of thanks to the Lord Mayor and the chairmen of the twelve major sub-committees on whose labours 'the great venture' had been founded. It was actually proposed as well that a testimonial be got up in recognition of the Lord Mayor's notable leadership. No one, at any time, had shown the slightest inclination to go looking for a scapegoat.[21]

There is no way of knowing whether or not Rhoscomyl attended the meeting of guarantors at the City Hall. His presence there would surely have put him to the test, for as his letter to J. Glyn Davies on 4 September shows he was certainly intent on nailing a scapegoat. The military man, for whom sound strategy and tactics precluded disasters in the field, had to conclude that someone had let his 'pardners' down. That someone was none other than G.P. Hawtrey, who had been lionized when 'the great venture' reached its back-slapping conclusion. In his review of the Pageant for *The Nationalist,* Hawtrey noted the serious shortage of advance bookings as the prime cause of the financial failure:

> As a general rule when the opening day comes the money already taken for reserved seats is sufficient to cover expenses. But we fell short of this happy condition of things by considerably more than ten thousand pounds! The cautious Welsh would not book.[22]

Ten thousand pounds! 'Cautious' strikes one as a pretty restrained epithet in that context. It was an enormous shortfall in 1909.

Rhoscomyl however had his very own view on the matter. He believed that they could have done with a smaller cast and could have used the same costumes in many different scenes to reduce costs without loss of spectacle. But it was a shady pageant-master that he singled out for a startling attack:

As to the Pageant it would have been a record forever if only Hawtrey had been even a fairly average man, instead of the impossible beggar he was. *Privately* he was 'on the make', and had no more sense of truth, honour, or common honesty than an old fox in the gorse.

Hawtrey had turned Sir Marchant Williams and the editor of *The Western Mail* against what he, Rhoscomyl, was striving for but the members of the various committees had not been fooled:

> 'Per contra', all the committees turned around and backed me through thick and thin against Hawtrey, when at last they found him out, and said that the Pageant was gone up unless I could survive the rush. When right and left men were cracking up and women breaking down in hysterics, I got to bed twice a week, five hours each time. How they cursed Hawtrey then!

It is best we recognize his outburst as out and out 'Old Fireproof' talk which Rhoscomyl must have known would land him in court if repeated in public. He was sufficiently acquainted with Falstaff not to make that mistake.[23]

It is more than likely that the Statement of Accounts holds the explanation for Rhoscomyl's 'private' denunciation of Hawtrey. The Pageant-Master was paid £500 and his 'Assistant' (yes, assistant), £200. Hawtrey's contract stipulated that in addition to his fee he was also to receive 20% of any profit amounting to £1,000, and 10% of any profit over and above that sum. As things turned out, he received no more than his basic fee. If his shortcomings were as reprehensible as Rhoscomyl painted them, and known to so many, he would surely have been a target for journalistic disapproval, but no adverse criticism came his way and no doubts were cast on his honesty. Moreover, when he died on 17 August 1910, aged 64, leaving an estate valued at £378.15.3, he could hardly be accounted a man of means. But he had been paid more than twice as much as Rhoscomyl, the Pageant's historian, and Rhoscomyl would not have been slow to resent the higher value accorded to Hawtrey's contribution. Hence his self-promotion as the selfless, tireless activator whose genuine passion for his country's past had willed its celebration when Hawtrey's suspect behaviour threatened impending disaster. None but Rhoscomyl could have saved the day.[24]

Hawtrey, to the best of our knowledge, has left no account of his personal dealings with Rhoscomyl, but in his 'Foreword' to the *Book of the Words* there is a short paragraph that hints at an acrimony not of his making:

> Captain Owen Vaughan, otherwise 'Owen Rhoscomyl', was appointed to work with me. *So far as I am concerned* [my italics], the combination has been a most happy one. The result, *for good or evil,* will be seen in our work, for which we are conjointly responsible.[25]

Read in the light of Rhoscomyl's bitter letter to J. Glyn Davies it is what remains unsaid in that paragraph that speaks most clearly to us now. To resort to euphemism, Rhoscomyl was a 'difficult' man. His clear-sighted obituarist in *The Welsh Outlook* put it well when he said:

> Upon such a man, the restraints and conventions of modern society could never lie easily. He chafed under them, failed sometimes to understand them, and was, in consequence, betrayed into an impatience which it was easy to pardon.[26]

Easy for some, but not everyone, is the truth. It was his 'manner' that cost him the command of the 'Welsh Horse', that according to J. Glyn Davies resulted in him being denied the credit for the 'brilliant audacity' that brought about the Investiture of the Prince of Wales in 1911, and that also made him at times a less than winning publicist for Howard de Walden's fledgling 'National Theatre' in 1914. Sure of himself and prone to erupt, Rhoscomyl invariably saw his way clearly and was ever impatient to storm along it.

There is another possible reason for Rhoscomyl's condemnation of Hawtrey that should be considered. *The Times* had expected to see more fighting in the course of the Pageant and was disappointed to find Gwenllian and Glyndŵr featuring in battle-free scenes. To what extent *The Times* was aware of Rhoscomyl's warrior-dominated interpretation of Welsh history is a matter for conjecture, but given his life-long admiration for Glyndŵr it is surprising that his arch-hero's assumption of the title of Prince of Wales in 1400 was not one of the Pageant's episodes – indeed, the coruscating episode. As an author Rhoscomyl wrote nothing better than his chapter on Glyndŵr in *Flame-Bearers of Welsh History*, and his advocacy of Glyndŵr's right to be recognized as Wales's paramount champion was just as passionate in August 1913 when in *The Western Mail* he made out a case for his inclusion in the pantheon of ten heroes and one heroine whose statues were eventually unveiled in Cardiff's City Hall by David Lloyd George, MP, Secretary of State for War, on 27 October 1916: 'Wales is Wales today because of Glyndŵr. For that, and that alone, we set him high and keep his memory green . . . His was the labour: ours the benefit. Peace be with him, if we prove worthy.'[27]

Just as puzzling is the place allotted Llywelyn, the Last Prince of Wales (Llywelyn ein Llyw Olaf), in the Pageant. A pathos-ridden scene in the fourth interlude in which he leads his slaughtered bodyguard in silent procession before the grandstand seems a limp way of illustrating the 'one magnificent lesson' Rhoscomyl wanted people to take away with them, which was 'Never give in: keep fighting!' It would surely have been better grasped, and remembered for longer, had the last desperate stand by the legendary eighteen on Orewyn bridge across the river Irfon on 11 December 1282 been re-enacted. It would have been no more difficult to stage than Ivor Bach's assault on Cardiff Castle and it would have better served Rhoscomyl's warrior creed to show Llywelyn's bodyguard falling '[a]s men should end, proudly fighting'.[28]

Could it be that G.P. Hawtrey had denied Llywelyn and Glyndŵr the limelight that one would have expected Rhoscomyl to have planned for them? As pageant-master the responsibility for dramatizing the material provided by the historian was his, and in judging the usability of what was provided his opinion, despite his confessed ignorance of Welsh history, could be expected to carry most weight. In his letter to J. Glyn Davies excoriating Hawtrey, Rhoscomyl protested that the Pageant as staged in Cardiff was not as he had scripted it and was even further removed from what he had originally intended. Nevertheless, what had been seen in Sophia Gardens would not be bettered until he did so, in Swansea, the following year! He had in mind a pageant dramatizing 'The search for the Holy Grail' but nothing came of that. Rhoscomyl however was soon to find his Holy Grail in the Investiture of the Prince of Wales in 1911.

The possibilty that Hawtrey, for whatever reason, changed parts of the National Pageant as first conceived by Rhoscomyl is intriguing. According to *The Western Mail*, it had been Hawtrey's decision to include Hywel Dda, Ivor Bach, Gwenllian, Llywelyn Fawr, 'Fluellen' and Henry Tudor in the Pageant, but nothing was said about the thinking behind his choice. Interestingly, an appreciative journalist in *The Evening Standard* had drawn attention to the 'ticklish' business of deciding what tableaux should be selected, ticklish not only because of their 'abundance' but because of 'the desire underlying the whole undertaking that Welsh history should, once and for all, be truly stated and done justice to'. As if aware of tension between Hawtrey and Rhoscomyl he added: 'It was a big and delicate task, but they accomplished it admirably, and Wales will be still prouder of her past as the result of the remembrancers which these two men have included in the Pageant's cast.' We can only curse the want of a blueprint that might have shown how it had been Rhoscomyl's intention from the start to deliver a more militant public version of Welsh history than the one actually presented in Cardiff – one with Glyndwr, the undying Prince of Wales, as its kingpin.[29]

At the risk of overdoing conjecture while musing over the interlude placings allotted Llywelyn and Glyndŵr in the National Pageant – their scenes would not have exceeded four to five minutes in the first attempt of its kind to make Welsh history a living reality for the public at large – the restraints that might have been imposed by the active involvement of the members of several 'grand households' on what it was deemed proper to re-enact shouldn't go unremarked. As they had done in 1906 when Edward VII and his Queen visited Cardiff, rank and nobility came again in costumed splendour in 1909, dripping allegiance to the Crown and freighted with pride in the Empire. Such people would expect a celebration of Wales's past not to offend, let alone traduce, England's present.

While rejoicing in the historic integrity of Lord Tredegar's Welshness, it was of the greatest importance to revere him also as an aristocrat of British distinction. His valour in the Crimea had earned him the right to be acknowledged as a British hero 'pur sang'. When in 1909 his Lordship received the freedom of the city of Cardiff on Balaclava Day (25 October), Lord Mayor Lewis Morgan, who was soon to be selected by the Conservatives to contest the Parliamentary seat of south Glamorgan in 1910, had his eyes firmly on England as he praised him:

> 'It is a day that will never be forgotten in English history, and wherever Englishmen meet to-day, and wherever the English flag waves, people are reminded of the heroism shown, and the work done by you, my lord, and the noble Six Hundred on that memorable day at Balaclava. We can join with them in saying, 'When can their glory fade?'[30]

No, it could certainly not be expected for Lord Tredegar, as Owen Glyndwr, to remind England forcibly of its history of oppression in Wales. 'Good form' dictated otherwise.

Equally interesting as a Welshman of impeccable pedigree was Mr Morgan Stuart Williams of St Donat's Castle, who played the part of Llywelyn the Great in the Pageant. He could boast descent from the famous Williams family of Aberpergwm in the Neath valley. His son,

Godfrey, who with his wife played the parts of Owen Tudor and Catherine, the widow of Henry V, lived in Aberpergwm at the time of the Pageant, and his nephew, Rhys Williams, the Pageant's king of the Silures, lived at Miskin Manor. Welsh to the core, they were nevertheless educated to meet the requirements of upper-class English mores and values. Less than a week before donning his Pageant costume, Rhys Williams had played host at Miskin Manor to Her Royal Highness, Princess Louise and her husband, the Duke of Argyll,

MR RHYS WILLIAMS, MISKIN MANOR

during their visit to south Wales where they had previously, in 1908, enjoyed the hospitality of Morgan Williams at St Donat's Castle, as had Princess Christian of Schleswig-Holstein and her daughter, Princess Victoria, in 1905. Such splendidly connected Welsh people were hardly likely to appear in a National Pageant bristling with resentment, no matter how far removed in time, towards England.[31]

When Morgan Stuart Williams died on 13 December 1909 at the age of 64, much was made of his birth at Aberpergwm in 1845, and of his proud use of the Welsh language as spoken by the 'gwerin' of Morgannwg (Glamorgan) and of his love for the folk tunes his aunt, Maria Jane Williams of Aberpergwm, had secured for posterity in her famous collection of *Ancient National Airs of Gwent and Morgannwg* published in 1844. St Donat's Castle, where he made his home in 1900, boasted an unmistakable Welsh ethos, proof of his abiding interest in history, antiquities and armoury – a subject on which he was held to be an authority. Morgan Williams qualified as a 'traditional' Welsh aristocrat – and more.

Mr Morgan Stuart Williams as 'Llywelyn Fawr'

Educated at Eton and Peterhouse, he was a Conservative who counted Disraeli as a personal friend. His status as a wealthy landowner and industrialist saw him appointed High Sheriff of Glamorgan in 1875. The vicar of Aberpergwm (the Pageant's Dewi Sant) in his eulogy of him talked of a patriot every bit as iconic as David Lloyd George, before adding a final coat of lustre to his distinction with these words: 'Patriotic Welshman though he was, he was none the less a good Englishman. He had distinguished himself at Cambridge, and was, as befitted a man of his status in society, a cultivated English gentleman.'[32]

Quite simply, it would never do for Llywelyn and Glyndŵr, as native warrior Princes of Wales, to act in a manner likely to provoke in any of the onlookers feelings of resentment, or shame, or anger at the thought of conquest and subjugation. Whatever Rhoscomyl may have originally intended for them, it was Llywelyn's lot in the Pageant to appear as a bloodied mute, and Glyndŵr was limited to commanding his standard-bearers to shake out his banner as Prince of Wales, followed by 'the old war flag of the Cymry' – the Red Dragon. Flag-waving, with Lord Tredegar to the fore, was not only admissible, it was hugely popular, and it was another banner-raising, commendably civilized Glyndŵr that the dramatist, Beriah Gwynfe Evans, fashioned for the Investiture celebrations at Caernarvon in 1911 – a native Prince of Wales so nobly motivated that he could subsequently be paraded on a London stage. What truly mattered, as Rhoscomyl made clear in *The Book of the Investiture*, was that Wales should profit by another blaze of pageantry, that the ceremony at Caernarvon should be a mark 'to all the world that Wales is a special country in the Empire . . .' and was to be 'a land to which the Empire may look for help and strength in the hour of temptation and in the day of danger. Cymru am byth!'[33]

With people of high rank and quality featuring so prominently in the management and performance of the National Pageant, their presence must have tempered any urge to magnify the valour of 'rebel' Welsh princes in their struggles for freedom against 'the English'. Wales and England wed was to be the providential end of the story and it was in view from the moment 'Dame Wales' led her attendant ladies out of the castle for the prologue. Loyalty to Wales had to be seen as a national strength that, when dedicated to the service of the Empire, inevitably became a higher, more ennobling and rewarding virtue. That most certainly was the view from above, and as various press reports and E.A. Morphy's *Pictorial and Descriptive Souvenir* make clear, the Pageant was unmistakably a top-down venture imbued with upper-crust and middle-class attitudes and expectations. The organizing commitees were obviously the male preserve of 'worthy citizens'; the regiments of women who toiled to produce myriad costumes were marshalled by ladies. *The Western Mail* knew what it was about when it lavished adjectives on the fashionably attired spectators in the grandstand on the opening day of the Pageant. The 'best people' had to set the tone.

Notwithstanding the need for crowd-pulling spectacle and excitement, a sense of propriety was still 'de rigeur' – a fact illustrated by the Lord Mayor's appreciation of the way Ivor Bach's rugby-playing warriors had conducted themselves, and Rhoscomyl's praise for the behaviour of the soldiers once released from their parts as 'Ruffians'. Indeed, the mass of Pageant spectators behaved as impeccably as any National Eisteddfod throng. No one was arrested for drunkenness or general loutishness. For Louis Napoleon Parker, 'a Pageant is absolutely democratic', and Edward Thomas (Cochfarf) had wanted The National Pageant of Wales to be seen as the product of 'a democracy of patriots'. The fact remains, however, that its whole ethos was determined by the 'notable leaders of society' who wanted nothing as much as the promotion of Wales within Britain. *The Evening Standard* greeted the Pageant as 'a democracy bent on proving their entity as a separate nation, though by no means devoid of that spirit of loyalty to the British throne which, as much as anything else, has helped them to their share in the building up and the maintenance of the British Empire'. As for the domination of the chief parts by 'the high-placed people of Wales', their 'self-sacrificing efforts and personal presence amongst the performers' (as mistakenly believed in the event) couldn't fail 'to swell the bookings for the higher-priced seats throughout the fortnight'. 'Noblesse oblige' came in many forms.[34]

Given their triumphalist coverage of The National Pageant of Wales it is not surprising that Cardiff's major newspapers – the editors of *The Western Mail* and *The South Wales Daily News* had served on the Pageant's committees – were reluctant to publicize the financial failure of 'the great venture'. Both papers refrained from editorial comment after the meeting of guarantors at the City Hall on 8 November. It was one thing to celebrate 'the magnificent manner in which they had kept up the reputation of "dear old Cardiff" for thoroughness of purpose'. It was another thing altogether to broadcast that all the talents deployed, all the effort expended by thousands of people, had failed to clear the costs involved in staging what had confidently been predicted would be an incontestable demonstration of 'the worthiness of Wales'. Trumpeted far and wide as a 'National', as opposed to a 'local' Pageant, the financial loss underscored what must have been difficult to stomach – which was that a large part of the nation, the Welsh-speakers of west and north Wales, had not flocked to Cardiff. They literally kept their distance and were hardly encouraged to give their support by a Welsh-language press that gave 'the great venture' little more than cursory attention.

Despite the central involvement of Cardiff's Cymrodorion from the outset, despite the clear support of prominent 'Cymru Fydd' proponents such as W. Llewelyn Williams, MP, and E.T. John, MP, and despite the enthusiastic participation of a historian as well-regarded as Howell T. Evans, the Welsh-speaking scholarly fraternity in general were uncommitted. Professor John Rhŷs, who had written approvingly of Rhoscomyl's *Flame-Bearers of Welsh History*, seems not to have seen the Pageant; his reaction, if he did, was certainly not reported in the press. And to re-emphasize what is so difficult to understand, O.M. Edwards said not a word about the Pageant in his popular periodical,

Cymru, and must have chosen to stay away from Sophia Gardens, as did J.E. Lloyd. Even Rhoscomyl's staunch friend, J. Glyn Davies, had nothing to say, publicly at least, about what had been done in Cardiff.

At a time when Edwards's *Cymru* found space for poems of all kinds and when the equally popular periodical, *Y Geninen* (The Leek), positively teemed with poetry on every conceivable (acceptable) subject, The National Pageant of Wales went unsung. (Would that the bards had remained just as silent in 1911 when the Investiture dredged from them a slew of witless rhymings in Welsh and English.) Are we to read into this silence nothing more than a resentment of Cardiff's recent promotion from industrial boom town to anglophile British city? Mayors and Mayoresses in Wales were invited to the luncheon provided for the Lord Mayor, the Lady Mayoress and sundry Sheriffs of London at the City Hall on Saturday 31 July. From north Wales the Mayor of Wrexham alone chose to attend, while from the west they came from Carmarthen, Kidwelly, Haverfordwest, Pembroke and Cardigan. It was not a particularly impressive demonstration of widespread Welsh pride. There was clearly a substantial measure of antipathy between north and south Wales. The subversion of the 'Cymru Fydd' movement in the infamous Newport meeting of the Liberal Federations in 1896 still rankled in the north and west, and the decision to take the Investiture of the Prince of Wales away from Cardiff's swagger and wealth to Caernarvon's raw past had, in the opinion of dismissive Cardiffians, more than a suspicion of 'touché' about it. That was Lloyd George country for sure.[35]

Strangely for a Welsh-language press never slow to stoke controversies and encourage blistering arguments, the Pageant suffered no destructive mass attacks. In *Y Brython* (The Briton) a columnist going by the name of 'Brenni Brown' dismissed the Pageant's pseudo-patriotism and was supported by 'Siluriad II', who objected to its pronounced militarism. 'Brenni Brown' saw fit to preach that patriotism was no mere toy and if a nation could not keep in memory the bravery and sacrifice of its heroes without resort to some sort of exhibition, it were best forgotten. Moreover, Cardiff's pageanteers cared but little for the history of Wales, thinking more of their own appearance than of the fate of those similarly garbed centuries ago:

> *Eithr hawdd gwybod, wedi'r cyfan, mai ysbryd ysgafn, arwynebol, yr ugeinfed ganrif sydd yn y galon – yr ysbryd hwnnw a feddwl mwy am rodres allanol nag am ddyheadau dyfnion y fynwes wir wladgarol.* (But it is easy to detect, after all, that the spirit in the heart is the frivolous, superficial spirit of the twentieth century – that spirit which thinks more of external show than of the deepest desires in the truly patriotic heart.)[36]

Awakened from their slumbers the heroes of old would surely laugh uproariously to see some of them represented by bespectacled, skinny youths.

It was a short, barbed rejection of a National Pageant whose promoters held such high hopes for the good results its restorative powers would have in a land too long depressed by fears of entrenched inferiority, and it is of a piece with a satirical send-up of anglophile social climbers, entitled *'Pla yr Epaod'* (The Plague of the Apes), by yet another pseudonymous writer calling himself 'Owain Glyn Dŵr'. It appeared in *Y Geninen* in October 1909, and while not actually singling out the Pageant for derision, its content and tone leave little room to doubt that the recent Sophia Gardens 'extravaganza' would have whetted 'Owain Glyn Dŵr's' blade. What must have been Rhoscomyl's thoughts on reading such stuff in *Y Brython* and *Y Geninen*? Whatever they were, he did not make them public. No one took up the cudgels on behalf of what had been a genuinely ground-breaking National Pageant. In the Welsh-language press it seems to have been allowed to float away on an ebbtide of general unconcern.[37]

Perhaps that shouldn't have come as too much of a surprise, for at the National Eisteddfod held in the Royal Albert Hall in London, 15-18

June, with all the great and the good of Wales in attendance, a tremendous opportunity to publicize 'the great venture' was lost. Admittedly, the ever alert A.W Swash had 'papered' the hall with pageant-promoting explanatory literature and posters, but no one took to the platform to tell the huge audience about what was soon to happen in Cardiff, let alone to impress upon them, with all the guns of eisteddfod oratory blazing, that it had to succeed, that the good reputation of Wales had to be enhanced. Some soon-to-be pageanteers took to the stage as day presidents, none more distinguished than Lord Tredegar and Lord Mostyn, but they let the opportunity slip. So did the mercurial David Lloyd George, MP, who, as Chancellor, would be too caught up in the toils of his 'People's Budget' to visit the Pageant. He, more than anyone, could have enthused his audience and sent them flocking to Cardiff, but he chose instead to urge the National Eisteddfod not to make a habit of forsaking its invigorating mountain home in Wales for the glossy attractions of city life – no matter how great the city![38]

It was left to The Right Honourable Arthur J. Balfour, MP, and Prime Minister Asquith, in their role as day presidents, to emphasize the importance of encouraging 'local patriotism', which they did without indicating that they had any inkling of what was soon to be staged in Sophia Gardens, let alone challenging the Welsh to better the York Pageant managed by Louis Napoleon Parker, which would run concurrently with the Cardiff venture. Not only was the importance of The National Pageant of Wales not broadcast from the Royal Albert Hall's stage, it was not even made the subject of a lecture in one of the heavyweight 'Cymmrodorion Section' meetings, when none other than Lord Tredegar was President of that Honourable Society, and when the readily supportive historian, W. Llewelyn Williams, MP, or the perennially crusading Sir Marchant Williams were on hand to accomplish the task. Talk about sins of omission!

The two publicists who should have appeared on the Royal Albert Hall stage, of course, were Rhoscomyl and Edward Thomas (Cochfarf).

They had forayed together into different parts of south Wales to beat the drum for the Pageant, Cochfarf as stirring in Welsh as Rhoscomyl was passionate in English. But the 1909 National Eisteddfod clashed with preparations for rehearsals in Sophia Gardens and the latter would have had the first claim on their time. Nevertheless, a day's return train journey from Cardiff to London with the express purpose of promoting the Pageant on the Royal Albert Hall stage was perfectly feasible. Distance wasn't the problem: it is much more likely that the National Eisteddfod managers would have been disinclined to let Rhoscomyl unleash a typically patriotic harangue in a place that had assumed the character of an English imperial temple. They already knew they would have to repulse suffragette sorties; to have to contain a Rhoscomyl charge as well would have been too exhausting!

From what has already been said about him in this book, it shouldn't be difficult to accept that Rhoscomyl was by nature a confrontational man, one who would say what he had to say no matter what the place or who the company. He prided himself on being, 'pace' the cliche, 'his own man', ploughing his own furrow with nonconforming self-certainty. Steve Attridge has noted how his 'highly personalized ideas on warfare' distanced him from the practices of the regular army whose 'regimented militarism' bred 'clockwork officers', unworthy of respect. Preaching self-reliance as a cardinal virtue, Rhoscomyl's invocation of 'manliness' in *Old Fireproof* acquired 'an almost transcendent status, hence the frequent references to the Captain as god-like, mysterious, endowed with extraordinary uncompromising physical and moral powers'. Yes, Rhoscomyl did see himself as a kind of superior being – a breed of superior Welsh patriot for sure.[39]

It was J. Glyn Davies who said of him: 'Men of action are disconcerting beings, and Rhoscomyl was cyclonic.' 'Cyclonic' as an adjective befitting its subject was a palpable hit. It was Davies, too, who best succeeded in communicating something of his unrelenting, alienating determination to coerce people into a collaborative position:

He fastened on his man, paralysed him, came straight to the point, and demanded that he should put his Welsh nationalism into action. And usually that was the last that Rhoscomyl saw of him; it took him a long time to realise how thin a veneer symbolical nationalism was in others.[40]

It is easy to understand that such an approach, coming from an outsider of uncertain background and meagre means, would be ill received by those who adjudged themselves his betters, socially and educationally. To be accused of moral cowardice and sycophancy, as had been the lot of Rhoscomyl's audience in Manchester in February 1909, would be intolerable in the Royal Albert Hall. In Manchester he had recounted his experience of some English tourists in a hotel in a Welsh town who, drinking whisky and smoking cigars after a large dinner, decided to 'send for the people to sing for us'. Rhoscomyl exploded:

> . . . send for them as they would not send for Kaffirs. Can you go lower than that – to be called upon to sing your national songs for the pleasure of English visitors. I made up my mind then that when I came back I would do what I could to stop that at any rate. It is your own fault that you are treated in this way. You accept the English history and estimate of your race. You read English books; you won't buy Welsh books. No man ever wrote a Welsh history and got back his expenses. It is our own fault.[41]

That was no kind of language for a National Eisteddfod platform in the Royal Albert Hall in 1909. And it was probably his patriotic aggressiveness that kept Rhoscomyl out of the circle of the Gorsedd of Bards, for had he been offered entry into the Druidic fraternity his romantic cast of mind and love of pageantry would have prompted immediate acceptance. The bards, aware of his contempt for Matthew Arnold's advocacy of fanciful, decorative Celticism, would no more expect him to shout 'Heddwch!' unfailingly than they would expect a hawk to chirp.

Had Rhoscomyl attended the National Eisteddfod in London he would, perhaps, have listened to the performance of Elgar's dramatic cantata, *Caractacus*, and possibly even found a way of introducing some feature of it into the Pageant's first episode. But far more important, he could have made personal contact with the two poets awarded the prime poetry prizes that year – the renowned T. Gwynn Jones, whose *awdl* in the traditional strict metres on *'Gwlad y Bryniau'* (The Land of the Hills) won him the Chair, and the firebrand W.J. Gruffydd, whose *pryddest* (a long meditative poem) on 'Yr Arglwydd Rhys' (Lord Rhys ap Gruffydd, 1132-97) won him the Crown. They might even have been induced to write in support of the Pageant, which, given the high regard in which they were held on account of their steadfast Welshness as much as their literary talents, would have been no small thing. Both their prizewinning poems in 1909 had their roots in myth and history, and T. Gwynn Jones's *'Gwlad y Bryniau'* in particular was filled, if not to the same degree, with the mythopoeic power that made his 1902 'awdl', 'Ymadawiad Arthur' (The Passing of Arthur), a memorable harbinger of a literary revival.

Rhoscomyl would have identified with the warrior spirit that drove both poets to attack the hypocrisy, sycophancy, self-denial and widespread anglophilia they saw corroding Welsh life, and that in 1902 spurred T. Gwynn Jones to write two withering sonnets of contempt for a people whose 'determination' to erect, through public subscription, a towering statue in memory of Llywelyn, the Last Prince of Wales, amounted after fifty years of exhortation to less than £200. There is, however, no reason to believe that either of these two significant literary figures were attracted by the National Pageant, certainly not to the extent that they felt a need to write about it. One can only regret that T. Gwynn Jones's operatic muse wasn't brought to bear on 'the great venture' in Sophia Gardens. His *'Gwlad y Bryniau'* would long outlast the Pageant in public memory, but had he written about it, in either eulogistic or satiric mode, he would surely have secured its right to be remembered and prized for its uniqueness. The National Pageant of Wales by any reckoning was, and still remains in retrospect, a quite remarkable exercise in the public use of history in modern Wales.

To claim for it a marked success in promoting a general interest in Welsh history would, however, be to overstate its importance. Some of its more robust promoters expected it to trigger a lively involvement with the past. They were confident that it would bring many spectators into a genuinely imaginative relationship with historical events and characters. Enthusiasts such as A.T. Davies, the Secretary of the Welsh Department of the Board of Education; Sir Marchant Williams; W. Llewelyn Williams, MP, and E.T. John, MP, expected sound educational benefits to stem from the undeniable success they claimed had been achieved. A.T. Davies had heard 'history speaking in living tones' and urged Wales's intermediate schools to enact mini-pageants based on the periods of Welsh history they had been studying:

> the result would be that a new educational force would arise in our land, which would foster a greater patriotism, which would reflect itself in a quickened national life, and all that results from it.[42]

Sir Marchant thought the Pageant, as an object-lesson in Welsh history, had been 'simply invaluable'. For him it was:

> the beginning of a revolution in the attitude of the Welsh people towards the legitimate drama as something that serves to bring the distant past visibly before the eyes of the people.[43]

W. Llewelyn Williams was prepared to overlook a few factual errors because the Pageant breathed 'the spirit of romance and adventure' which made Welsh history 'the most fascinating in the world to students who have a touch of imagination and fancy'. Moreover, it would:

make all of us feel prouder of Wales and of her storied past, and by emphasizing our common pride of heritage it should help to bring all classes more together.[44]

As for E.T. John, who would talk at the drop of a hat about the debt owed by the Empire to the Welsh, he was sure that the Pageant had brought 'the essence of the history of Wales' before the public for the first time and he was equally sure of the gains that would follow:

> Welsh history will have many devoted students in the next twenty years, and where few have been labouring in the past many will be labouring in the future.
>
> I look forward to the time when honours in our Welsh University will be far more easily attained, and that result will be due, in my opinion, to the very admirable Pageant which we have witnessed.[45]

Such sanguine expectations, voiced as they were in the dizzying, self-congratulatory aftermath of the Pageant, are perfectly understandable. It had been a great show for patrician and commoner alike. Welsh history in costume had been exciting, thrilling, even instructive. And 'padgeing' had been good fun. But it was much too soon to think of extending the teaching of Welsh history in schools and colleges in any meaningful sense. Dr Naunton Davies, whose ambition it was to write 'a Welsh National romance' featuring Llywelyn the Last Prince of Wales at its heart, argued that the Pageant would have served little purpose if it did not encourage writers to flesh out Welsh history in captivating books. His own experience to date had been unrewarding. His countrymen ignored his work, leaving it 'to Englishmen and English critics to discover its existence'.[46] Buried in the maw of England's imperial story, it would take a further half century for the history of Wales to emerge, Jonah-like, into the light provided by a battery of historians whose extensive research, methodologies, critical faculties and vision would elevate the study of

Welsh history to the heights attained in the second half of the twentieth century.

As late as 1963 J.F. Rees, who in *The Welsh Leader* in 1905 had protested against the 'footnote-to-English-history' approach to Welsh history, still regretted the marginal position that their national history occupied in the lives of the Welsh people. He spoke plainly:

> The appeal to history, which has been such a powerful influence in stimulating consciousness of nationality (as, for instance, in Czecho-Slovakia), has not had a similar effect in Wales. The history of Wales as related by competent historians is well worthy of study, but it is a tangled story and its lessons are not simple. It does not afford the basis for uncritical glorification of the past. Those who seek flame-bearers of Welsh nationhood are apt to burn their fingers.[47]

It surely says something about the vigour of Rhoscomyl's writing that a professional historian of Rees's calibre thought fit to single him out for disapproval in a book published in 1963. As a matter of fact Rhoscomyl's approach to historiography, his belief in the soundness of those 'infernal pedigrees' as the key to releasing the 'facts' about early Welsh history, did not long outlast him.

Following Rhoscomyl's death in 1919, Lord Howard de Walden offered the University of Liverpool £250 to establish a research fellowship 'for the study of the oldest Welsh genealogies begun by the late Colonel A.O. Vaughan, D.S.O.' The offer was accepted. From 1920 to 1923 the fellowship was held by Gwilym Peredur Jones, a Birkenhead-born student who graduated with First Class Honours in Medieval History in 1914, followed by a MA degree in 1916. The son of the editor of *Y Brython*, known simply throughout Wales as 'J.H.', Gwilym Peredur Jones already held the Charles Beard Fellowship, 'the highest distinction available in medieval history'. He was to be the first and only recipient of the Lord Howard de Walden Fellowship in Celtic. He was subsequently to distinguish himself as a Professor of Economic

History at Sheffield University – far removed from Rhoscomyl's genealogical interests. In 1954 he wrote to Olwen Vaughan confirming her impression of her father as a 'romantic idealist', adding that he had 'near the centre of his conviction' a 'rejection of the popular, and mistaken, view that the Welsh were merely the descendants of beaten Britons fleeing, before triumphant Anglo-Saxons, to the West'. Nothing would shake his belief that they were, in fact, 'the offspring of men who came as conquerors, from the North, in the wake of retreating Romans'. As for Rhoscomyl's obsession with genealogy, he laughingly disposed of it by telling Olwen that a friend of his, one Edward Owen, on seeing a proof copy of *The Matter of Wales* when he was recovering from an illness, started to think that 'the sickness had affected his brain!' The furrow Rhoscomyl had started to plough was not about to be extended by any acolytes.[48]

It comes as no surprise that the historians who transformed the study of Welsh history in the twentieth century, starting with (Sir) J.E. Lloyd, passed Rhoscomyl by, given that the National Pageant of 1909 was never thought worthy of a serious historian's attention. For example, major works such as Kenneth O. Morgan's *Rebirth of a Nation; Wales 1880-1980* (1981); Gwyn A. Williams's *When was Wales?* (1985); R.R. Davies's magisterial *The Revolt of Owain Glyn Dŵr* (1995) and Geraint H. Jenkins's *A Concise History of Wales* (2007) make no mention of him, while John Davies in his notable *Hanes Cymru* (A History of Wales in Welsh) (1990) merely refers in less than a sentence to his overheated expectations after the Tudor victory on Bosworth Field, and Dai Smith in *Wales: A Question for History* (1999) notes 'his sacral drive' as the historian of the Pageant, which is snappily seen off as an 'overblown Edwardian fantasy'. The advances of scholarship would have proved unstoppable and irrefutable for a living Rhoscomyl. Dead, the status accorded him by the likes of Sir Marchant Williams in *The Nationalist* would soon be lowered. He was destined to become a footnote.

Rhoscomyl, while resenting his demotion, would not have been surprised by it had he lived. He obviously sensed that for many of his influential contemporaries in Wales there was something frankly 'outré' about his involvement with Welsh life and culture. He knew himself to be an outsider, as J. Glyn Davies testified, and his resentment acted as a whetstone for his nationalism, which he must have considered a superior brand to that which resulted in the 'Cymru Fydd' debacle in 1896. He won no friends by making public his contempt for '"dilettante" nationalism', insisting that it was 'time to lift the spear against those "ardent nationalists" who are in the business of nationalism for what they can get out of it'. By laying himself open to a charge of arrogating to himself a superior pride in nationality he was limiting his ability, as well as his opportunities, to energize the Welsh will to succeed. And there was nothing that he wanted to promote as much as a determined, confident, self-reliant Wales. He yearned to be an insider, telling his audience in Manchester in February 1909 that he favoured 'A National Pageant of Wales' as opposed to 'A Welsh National Pageant' because 'everyone living in Wales, doing his best for the country and the people, was entitled to the privilege of being represented by the pageant'. For him, '"Cymro" stood for comrade; it did not necessarily mean identity in race, but dwelling in common, living in the country and doing their best for it'. Rhoscomyl as an advocate for twenty-first century inclusivity? Resurrected, he might even have functioned as a PR man for 'Plaid' had it not discarded 'Cymru' and rejected the 'Triban' for a pallid yellow flower.[49]

Not unexpectedly, given the age he was born into and his own extraordinary life of regular and irregular soldiering, Rhoscomyl was hardly a forerunner of the political nationalists who founded Plaid Cymru in 1925. For him, Welsh nationalism was 'the determination to bring Wales to the front in the Empire in every way that offers'. It was essentially a force for helping Wales to catch up with the rest. He was a diehard royalist and an Empire man who had no ambition (certainly none declared) to unpick the constitutional settlement that had long since determined the position of Wales within the British state. Remember that in the Pageant it was the Welsh who petitioned

Henry VIII for an Act of Union. Rhoscomyl simply wanted the worthiness of Wales advanced with a crusading zeal by its people and fully recognized and appreciated by the ruling powers. It was his desire to bring an end to 'centuries of neglect', that is, centuries of disdain, that fired him to help bring about the Investiture of the Prince of Wales in 1911, a royal event that ironically released a flood of sycophancy in a country driven daft with gratitude for being so rewarded.[50]

Rhoscomyl was no sycophant. He held that Edward's Tudor ancestry made him a 'bona fide' Prince of Wales who could be served without in any way betraying the memory of Llywelyn and Glyndŵr. In bringing him to Caernarvon Castle to exchange vows of mutual loyalty and service with 'his people', Wales would be propelled into a favoured position within the Empire. Not for Rhoscomyl the image of a feminine Celtic Wales wedded to a masculine Aryan England. Rather he saw a warrior people sworn to follow a leader authenticated by their own history, who had likewise sworn to proclaim their worthiness and lead them on to greater things.

Not for nothing did more than ten thousand soldiers descend on Caernarvon for the Investiture, with three Welsh regiments taking pride of place among them. Not for nothing did 'The March of the Men of Harlech' resound throughout the ancient town. Not for nothing did Oxford University's professor of Celtic, Sir John Rhŷs, in reading the Loyalty Address of the Welsh People, emphasize the constancy of their support for England's expansionist wars:

> We are bound to the Throne of your forefathers by six centuries of a common past, by the memory of imperishable deeds in peace and war, and by our hopes of greater things to come. The bowmen and the pikemen of Wales followed the Black Prince to Cressy and Henry of Monmouth to Agincourt. Her sons have stood side by side with Englishmen on many a stricken field, facing equal danger, with no unequal courage.[51]

This was a celebration of imperial togetherness for the ages.

At the time, any suggestion that the Investiture of 1911 amounted to nothing more than a favour-seeking parade of Welsh deference would have met with a roar of denial – particularly from Rhoscomyl. Had he lived to witness Edward's abdication and subsequent pandering to fascism, perhaps he would have been cured of his romantic idealism. He surely would have been had fate decreed that he should live until 1969 to see Investiture pageantry travestied by a self-serving Secretary of State for Wales who would have taxed the talents of a Molière or a Dickens. Rhoscomyl should have lived to pass judgement on Lord Tonypandy.

It is safe to assume that he would have been attracted to Plaid Cymru as a means of stimulating patriotism. But his militarism would surely have turned him against the three 'arsonists' – Saunders Lewis, the Reverend Lewis Valentine and D.J. Williams – who sought to destroy the bombing school at Penyberth in the Lleyn Peninsula in 1936. Of course it is diverting to think of him battling with two contradictory responses – the one insisting on their immediate execution as traitors, the other urging their recruitment as saboteurs and guerrilla fighters given the likelihood of a Nazi invasion! But leaving aside politics for which he had little stomach, a resurrected Rhoscomyl stripped of his kitbag of Victorian imperialistic, militaristic and racist attitudes, would bring with him in 2009 something much more valuable than a vote: he would bring a passionate belief in the talents and abilities of the Welsh people, and in their democratic right to be masters in their own house. For him, it was 'the spirit that is abroad in a land that counts. It is the *now* that matters. What is done is done, it cannot be recalled. What is to be done, and what may be done, is what counts most.'[52]

Very soon, Wales will face yet another referendum to decide its fitness to turn its recently gained Assembly into a mature legislative Senedd properly empowered to govern Wales for the betterment of all its people. Already the detractors are gathering, the usual consortium of self-promoters, fear-mongers, doom-merchants and blank Welsh-bashers. As ever they will target the national psyche, that fraught thing that in 1997 came within a few gibes of unravelling and ensuring our continued subservience. At such a time we would do well to remember the Rhoscomyl who in his day spoke out against treating Wales like 'a mere back-yard of England or at least like an outlying farm, the whole profit of which was to be spent, not on improving itself, but on ornamenting the home estate'. And we would do well to ponder the words he wrote, a century ago, when in an article on 'Bosworth Field' he prophesied an end to the timidity that had held the Welsh back for too long:

> This day of timidity will pass; this day of looking to England for all light is passing already. Our own past will give us a truer light before the play's much older . . . It will be seen that whatever tends to make Welshmen prouder of themselves as Welshmen; whatever tends to help them to look the other races fearlessly in the eye, is worth spending money on, for without such pride in a race there is no ready and vigorously responsive strength in that race for the statesman to call upon at need, whether the need be one of peace or war.[53]

Rhoscomyl's historiography falls well short by today's standards; his spirit has nevertheless stood the test of time and nothing would benefit a vacillating people more today than an infusion of his determination, self-reliance and fearlessness. Rhoscomyl never doubted that a nation's reach should always aim to exceed its grasp.

What the National Pageant's promoters dearly hoped would result from what they insisted was an overwhelming success (debts notwithstanding), was no different from what the promoters of the National Eisteddfod at the Royal Albert Hall hoped for. Commendatory recognition for Wales, praise for an achievement that would have done any part of Britain – particularly England – proud. At the National Eisteddfod, David Lloyd George, MP, had hailed the appearance of Asquith and Balfour on stage as day presidents as a notable advance for the Welsh: 'It must eventually benefit Wales when the statesmen who guide the destinies of the Empire take a special interest in her institutions, her language and her people.' Balfour had even owned up to a small measure of Welsh blood in his veins, but for Prime Minister Asquith, despite presenting himself as 'an undiluted and unadulterated Englishman, without a single Celtic corpuscle in his composition', to champion 'local patriotism' and welcome a fairer treatment of Wales by the London press was advancement indeed.[54]

It was left to *The Western Mail*, as befitted its wholehearted support for the National Pageant, to voice the hopes of all who had promoted and played a part in 'the great venture'. Having in an editorial on 27 July rejoiced in three hours of pageantry that traced fifteen hundred years of history down to the day 'when Hen Walia was welded into one harmonious whole and took her place as a sister side by side with old England'; having also rejoiced in the passing of a time 'when the patriotic Welshman was regarded as somewhat of a crank, and when only a few bold spirits dared to show that they loved the language and the lore of their little motherland', *The Western Mail* on 7 August in an editorial entitled 'What the Pageant has done', asked the question that went to the heart of the matter:

> Wales has never yet been allotted by historians her due share in our island story. Will the Pageant change all that? Will it impress upon historians who dismiss Wales with an occasional reference that the Principality has played a considerable part in directing the destinies of Great Britain? At all events, nobody could have watched the Pageant unfolding itself, through the heroic clash of arms and the tender poetry of love and romance, without feeling that here was a vital, but only half-known and half-understood, part of the history of the Empire.

As a striking example of the age-old longing for recognition, for approval (still influencing our relationship with England today), that quotation merits a prominent position in any anthology of Welsh contributionism or exceptionalism.[55]

A rewarding answer soon came in the form of a poem, 'Wales: a Greeting', penned by Sir William Watson (1858-1935), a forgettable poet as things turned out. But in 1909 his praise for

> A people caring for old dreams and deeds,
> Heroic story, and far descended song . . .

was music to Welsh ears, and his rhetorical description of 'gallant little Wales' as England's unfailing ally in the face of danger a cause for national back-slapping. As if divining the approach of some great calamity in the 'dim clouds' brooding '[o]n Europe, east and west . . .', Watson proclaimed England's faith in the fighting dependability of the Welsh and their care for an Empire that was essentially a vehicle for the spreading of Christian goodness. His words were intoxicating:

>   . . . But we know
> That should they [the clouds] break in tempest on these shores
> You, that with differing blood, with differing spirit,
> Yet link your life with ours, with ours your fate,
> Will stand beside us in the hurricane,
> Steadfast, whatever peril may befall:
> Will feel no separate heartbeats from our own,
> Nor aught but oneness with this mighty Power,
> This Empire, that despite her faults and sins
> Loves justice, and loves mercy, and loves truth,
> When truly she beholds them; and who thus
> Helps to speed on, through dark and difficult ways,
> The ever climbing footsteps of the world.[56]

Such was the sense of gratitude in Wales for so ennobling a 'Greeting' that a prize of £2 was offered for a Welsh translation of it in the National Eisteddfod at Wrexham in 1912. The adjudicator, Rhoscomyl's champion Sir Marchant Williams, had 37 translations to read, and he awarded the prize to one of the most popular lyrical poets of the day, and many days to follow – none other than the pious,

OSMOND AND MANSELL NICHOL CARNE AS THE 'SONS OF BASSET'
(INTERLUDE 4, SCENE 1). OSMOND (SEATED) WAS KILLED IN BATTLE, 7 MAY 1917.
(by permission of Miss S. Crawshay)

nature-loving monarchist, Eifion Wyn.[57] Within two years the Welsh, with Rhoscomyl in the van, would enlist in their tens of thousands to fight for the Empire, and Eifion Wyn would put his muse to good patriotic use, urging the boys to follow the flag, glorifying death in battle and excoriating pacifist cowards. What The National Pageant of Wales had enacted in Sophia Gardens in the summer of 1909 would be re-enacted in Flanders fields and on the Western front from 1914 to 1918. The Pageant had been no mere exercise in dressing up and play-acting; through graphic, public use of history it had tried to make a loud statement about the right of Wales to be recognized and properly valued as a British, imperial asset. Exchanging costumes for uniforms, the Welsh then went on to war to prove that they meant what they said in Sophia Gardens and were prepared to die to prove it.

If only the same spirit could be rekindled when the Welsh, facing nothing more terrible than a referendum to determine their own future, their own standing in the world, are called upon to vote. Perhaps, recalling our capital city's dispiriting response to the referendum of 1997, it is time to think of staging another National Pageant before 2011 – this time in celebration of the multiple talents of Wales. With 'Lyn the Atom' to replace 'Dame Wales' what a statement it would make. Let a creative Rhoscomyl spirit speak aloud for a nation's advance. The battlefield, as it has been over the centuries, is the Welsh mind. We are long overdue a decisive victory.

25.

"THE NATIONAL PAGEANT OF WALES."
INTERLUDE V. SCENE 3.
HENRY VIII. AND THE ACT OF UNION BETWEEN ENGLAND AND WALES, A.D. 1535.

NOTES

FOREWORD

[1] J.F. Rees, *The Problems of Wales and Other Essays* (Cardiff, 1963), 28.
[2] Prys Morgan, 'The Clouds of Witnesses' in R. Brinley Jones, ed., *Anatomy of Wales* (Cowbridge, 1972), 40.
[3] R.R. Davies, 'On being Welsh: A Historian's Viewpoint', *Transactions of the Honourable Society of Cymmrodorion*, New Series IX (2003), 35-6.
[4] *The Western Mail*, 5 Aug. 1913, 5.
[5] Colin A.Gresham, 'The Harlech Pageant', *Journal of the Meirioneth Historical and Record Society,* IX (no. 1), 1981, 97-105.

PREVIEW

[1] *The Western Mail* (=WM), 5 July 1906, 4; 7 July 1906, 7.
[2] *The South Wales Daily News* (=SWDN), 18 July 1906, 4.
[3] WM, 18 July 1906, 5.
[4] WM, 24 July 1909, 9.
[5] SWDN, 21 Aug. 1906, 4; 22 Sept. 1906, 6.
[6] WM, 24 July 1909, 8.
[7] SWDN, 22 Sept. 1906, 4.
[8] SWDN, 26 Sept. 1906, 4.
[9] WM, 23 July, 1908, 5.
[10] WM, 2 Feb. 1909 ,5; E.A. Morphy, *The National Pageant of Wales, Pictorial and Descriptive Souvenir. Cardiff July 26th – August 7th 1909* (Cardiff, 1909.)

[11] G.P. Hawtrey and Owen Rhoscomyl, *The National Pageant of Wales. Book of the Words* (Cardiff, 1909: 3rd edition); WM, 16 June 1909, 5. See John Davies, *Cardiff and the Marquesses of Bute* (UWP, Cardiff, 1981), 30, 77-8. John Crichton Stuart, the 4th Marquiss of Bute (1881-1947) was a patriotic Scot who spoke Welsh fluently and patronized Welsh culture. He married Augusta Bellingham (1880-1947).

[12] E.A. Morphy, op.cit., 'Scenes of the Pageant' (unpaginated).

[13] ibid; SWDN, 27 July 1909, 10; 9 Aug. 1909, 5; Gareth Williams, *1905 And All That* (Llandysul,1991), 68-89.

[14] E.A. Morphy, op.cit; SWDN, reports from 28 July – 11 Aug. 1909; WM, reports from 27 July – 12 Aug.1909.

[15] SWDN, 2 Aug. 1909, 6-7; 4 Aug. 1909, 8.

THE PARKERIAN PAGEANT

[1] WM, 5 July 1906, 4

[2] ibid.

[3] ibid.

[4] Louis Napoleon Parker, *Several of My Lives* (London, 1928); *Dictionary of National Biography, 1941-50*, 651.

[5] Louis Napoleon Parker, op.cit., 'My Pageant Life', 277-303.

[6] Robert Withington, *English Pageantry: An Historical Outline, vol. 11* (New York, 1963: Reprinted Edition). See chapter 3, 'The Parkerian Pageant', 194-233; Louis Napoleon Parker, op.cit., 302.

[7] ibid., 279.

[8] ibid., 283-4.

[9] ibid., 289-90.

[10] Robert Withington, op.cit., 194-5, 203.

[11] ibid., 196, 206.

[12] *The Times*, 19 July 1909, 12; 22 July 1909, 8.

[13] Robert Withington, op.cit., 210-12; Louis Napoleon Parker, op.cit., 277-303.

[14] ibid., 297, 301; Robert Withington, op.cit., 218; Deborah Sugg Ryan, '"Pageantitis": Frank Lascelles' 1907 Oxford Historical Pageant, Visual Spectacle and Popular Memory', *Visual Culture in Britain*, vol. 8, no. 2 (2007), 67: 'As Joshua Esty says, pageants "were the Hollywood epics of their day, complete with ornate special effects and casts of thousands." The later cinema epics of D.W. Griffith and Cecil B. DeMille, with their huge casts, were reminiscent of pageant spectacles and it is also likely that, in turn, epic films influenced pageants.'

[15] WM, 2 Feb.1909, 5

[16] The University of North Carolina, Greensboro: George P. Hawtrey Papers 1908 – ca. 1909; G.P. Hawtrey, 'Foreword' to the *Book of the Words*, iii-iv.

[17] George P. Hawtrey Papers, 1908 – ca.1909; Louis Napoleon Parker, op.cit., 297;

[18] ibid., 284

[19] George P. Hawtrey Papers, 1908 – ca.1909.

[20] G.P. Hawtrey, 'Foreword', to the *Book of the Words*, iii-iv.

[21] WM, 5 Feb 1909; E.A. Morphy, op.cit., 'The Makers of the Pageant' (unpaginated).

OWEN RHOSCOMYL

[1] WM, 16 Oct. 1919,7; *The North Wales Chronicle* (=NWC), 24 Oct. 1919, 6; NLW MSS J Glyn Davies Papers (=J.Glyn Davies Papers).

[2] NLW MSS Arthur Owen Vaughan (Owen Rhoscomyl) Papers (=Rhoscomyl Papers), no. 38; *Cymru*, 57 (Rhagfyr 1919), 169.

[3] WM, 16 Oct. 1919, 7; *The Welsh Outlook* (=WO), VI (1919), 271-2.

[4] Rhoscomyl Papers, nos. 36, 56, 59; John H. Davies and Huw Price, 'A Hero fit for Wales', *Cambria*, 1 (no. 3), 1998, 24-30; WM, 19 Oct 1919. Richard Sutton describes Rhoscomyl's father as a stonemason who was killed when some rock fell on him. His death and the birth of his son were both registered on 16 Oct. 1863.

[5] Rhoscomyl Papers, nos. 9, 36, 59: Ibid., nos. 9, 36, 59; David Littler Jones, 'Who was Owen Rhoscomyl?', *Hel Achau*, 34 (Aug. 1991), 3-4.

[6] Owen Rhoscomyl, *Lone Tree Lode* (London, 1913), see 'Introduction'; idem., *A Scout's Story* (London, 1908), chapter 1, 1-16; WO, VI (1919), 271-2; WM, 19 Oct. 1989. Richard Sutton has him working in a Lancashire cotton-mill until he left for the United States of America as a sixteen-year-old.

[7] Rhoscomyl Papers, no. 9; *Lone Tree Lode*, 1, 17, 43, 151.

[8] WM, 16 Oct. 1919, 7; *The Nationalist*, (Feb. 1909), 5-6.

[9] Rhoscomyl Papers.

[10] Bryn Owen, *Owen Rhoscomyl and the Welsh Horse* (Palace Books, Caernarfon, 1990), 11-18.

[11] *A Scout's Story*, 87.

[12] ibid., 294.

[13] *Lone Tree Lode*, 112-3.

[14] *The Times*, 2 June 1896, 13; 29 June 1897, 4.

[15] Roland Mathias, *Anglo-Welsh Literature: An Illustrated History* (Poetry Wales Press, Bridgend, 1986), 68-9.

[16] Beriah Gwynfe Evans, 'Wales in Fiction' in Thomas Stephens, ed., *Wales To-day and To-morrow* (Cardiff, 1907), 335-9; WM, 20 Oct. 1919. Following Rhoscomyl's death, J.H. Evans, Allen Raine's brother, wrote appreciatively of him recalling the 'sweet lines' he wrote when she died. He was 'proud to remember Owen Rhoscomyl as one of the ardent admirers of her works, and with whom she sometimes corresponded on literary subjects'.

[17] Lieutenant-Colonel Sir Reginald Rankin, *A Subaltern's Letters to his Wife* (London, 1901), 102.

[18] ibid., 100-102.

[19] Bryn Owen, op.cit., 14; WM 16 Oct. 1919, 7.

[20] Bryn Owen, op.cit., 14-15; Captain Owen Vaughan (Owen Rhoscomyl), *Old Fireproof* (Being the Chaplain's Story) (London, 1906), 42.

[21] Bryn Owen, op.cit., 17; WM, 16 Oct. 1919, 7.

[22] Rhoscomyl Papers, no. 11.

[23] ibid., nos. 11, 18, 38.

[24] ibid., nos. 38, 39, 64 (pp. 4, 5, 6, 9, 11, 12, 15, 16, 21, 22)

[25] ibid., no.16.

[26] *Old Fireproof*, 114-15; WM, 26 March 1927, 8 in noting Catherine's death on 25 March provides an alternative dramatic account of her first confrontation with Rhoscomyl. A fearless horsewoman, and a relative of President Kruger, she acted as a dispatch rider for the Boers. Galloping to the aid of some beleagured compatriots under attack by Rhoscomyl, she refused to draw rein when ordered to stop. Rhoscomyl promptly shot the horse from under her and quickly recovering from the shock of discovering that the rider was a woman, he just as quickly fell for her.

[27] *Old Fireproof*, 115.

[28] Rhoscomyl Papers, no. 16.

[29] *Old Fireproof*, 41; Bryn Owen, op.cit., 25.

[30] ibid., 26, 37.

[31] Rhoscomyl Papers, no. 21; WM, 23 Aug. 1923, 9.

[32] Rhoscomyl Papers, nos. 17, 20, 21; *Cymru*, 57 (Rhagfyr 1919), 169; WM, 20 Oct. 1919: That the demanding militarist was quick to recognise the ordinary soldier's needs and respond generously is beyond doubt. F.L. Beddoe, an ambulance driver during the Great War, remembered seeing him in Bethune when he was a major. As a Cardiffian who had met Rhoscomyl briefly during the Pageant, he ventured to approach him and talked with him at length about Wales before Rhoscomyl, noting his sorry appearance 'crusted with the mud and blood of the battle of the Somme', decided to refresh him after Beddoe had explained that his quarter master had no new uniforms to issue: 'I was taken to his billet, had a bath – what a change after days of washing in cold tea from a "dixie" – a good feed, a brand new wardrobe, an inquiry if I needed money, an invitation to call upon him at Dinas Powis when the days of peace came, and a farewell word of Welsh – and that is the last I saw of "Owen Rhoscomyl" in this flesh; but the memory of this simple act of kindness is with me until the last reveille.'

[33] SWDN, 5 Sept. 1884, 2.

[34] *National Eisteddfod Association Annual Report, 1886*, 32; *Wales* (ed. J. Hugh Edwards), April 1912, 199.

[35] WM, 1 Feb. 1887, 2.

[36] ibid., 6 June 1887, 5-6.

37 ibid., 29 April 1889, 2.

38 SWDN, 29 Sept. 1886, 3.

39 A.W. Wade-Evans, 'The Teaching of Welsh History in Welsh Schools', *The Welsh Leader*, 6 April 1905, 449-51.

40 ibid.

41 J. Fred Rees, B.A., 'The History of Wales: Its Nature', *The Welsh Leader*, 17 August 1905, 764-5. *Wales* (ed. O.M. Edwards) (1895), 53-5: 'But, so far, the senate of the University has done everything in its power to prevent the study of Welsh history and Welsh literature in Wales.'

42 Nancy Stepan, *The Idea of Race in Science: Great Britain 1800-1960* (London, 1982).

43 Hugh A. MacDougal, *Racial Myth in English History* (University Press of New England, 1982), Chapter 5 'A Myth Triumphant', 89-103.

44 *The Times*, 8 Sept. 1866.

45 *The Welshman*, 4 Sept. 1863.

46 *Carnarvon and Denbigh Herald*, 5/12 Sept. 1863.

47 Thomas Nicholas, *The Pedigree of the English People* (London,1867), 550, 552.

48 *Cymru Fydd*, 1 (Ebrill 1888), 194; *The Cambrian News*, 7 March 1879, 2; WM, 5 March 1879, 4.

49 B.B. Woodward, B.A., *The History of Wales from the Earliest Times* (London, 1853), 586-91.

50 *Archaeologia Cambrensis*, VII (1876), 323-36.

51 ibid., 329.

52 J.W. Burrow, *A Liberal Descent. Victorian historians and the English Past* (CUP, 1981), 191-2.

53 J.A. Froude, *The English in Ireland in the Eighteenth Century*, vol. 1, (London, 1887), 2-3, 9-10.

54 E.G. Millward, *Cenedl o Bobl Ddewrion* (Llandysul, 1991).

55 *Cyfansoddiadau Buddugol Eisteddfod Dinbych 1860 a'r Beirniadaethau* (Dinbych, 1863), 5; *Cambrian Journal*, IV (1857), 233-4

56 Hywel Teifi Edwards, *Codi'r Hen Wlad yn ei Hôl 1850-1914* (Llandysul, 1989), 187-237.

57 R.J. Derfel, *'Cymru yn ei chysylltiad ag Enwogion'*, *Y Traethodydd*, XI (1855), 322-59.

58 ibid., 336-7, 356.

59 ibid., 357.

60 Howell T. Evans, 'Llywelyn Bren', *The Nationalist*, (January, 1910), 17, Rhoscomyl Papers, no. 64.

61 Rhoscomyl, 'Gerald the Cymro', *The Nationalist*, (October1908), 7-12; idem., 'The Celtic Temperament', ibid., Feb.1909, 13-18.

62 *Old Fireproof*, 1-3, 18.

63 Rhoscomyl, 'Bosworth Field', *The Nationalist*, May 1908, 19; ibid., Feb. 1909, 12-13; *The Manchester Guardian*, 22 Feb. 1909, 14.

[64] Owen Rhoscomyl, *Flame-Bearers of Welsh History* (Merthyr Tydvil, 1905: School Edition), see 'Preface'.

[65] ibid., 253.

[66] Owen Rhoscomyl, 'The Place of Wales in the Empire', *Wales* (ed. J. Hugh Edwards), II (1912), 369-71.

[67] *Old Fireproof*, 25.

[68] Rhoscomyl, 'The Place of Wales in the Empire', 369-71. Rhoscomyl even saw the Investiture of the Prince of Wales in 1911 as the triumph of a people who had withstood all attempts not simply to crush them into submission but to exterminate them. They had nevertheless prevailed: 'I see the Cymry standing to the shock, see them still fighting on deathlessly, resolute to be Cymry, to dream their own dreams and to live their own lives, indomitable that Cymru shall be Cymru still.' (WM, 13 July 1911)

[69] *Old Fireproof*, 363; WM, 31 July 1909, 8: It seems inevitable that the Pageant area on Friday night, 30 July, should have been given over to hundreds of Boy Scouts for an 'exposition of mimic warfare' in the course of which they 'went through the evolutions with soldierlike bearing and precision . . . A camp was pitched and fires lit, with other accompaniments of camp life. The prevailing silence was broken upon by distant shots and war whoops and a desperate battle ensued with men dressed as Indians . . . The manoeuvres, which were followed with keen interest, concluded with the tableau "Guarding the Flag" and the singing of the National Anthem.' As the founder of the Scouts, Baden Powell, as another hero of the Boer War, would have been well pleased by Rhoscomyl's encouragement of them during the National Pageant fortnight.

[70] *Old Fireproof*, 364.

[71] *ibid.*, 388.

[72] WM, 22 Dec. 1899, 6; *The Graphic*, 61 (3 Feb. 1900), 178.

[73] Owen Rhoscomyl, 'The National Pageant of Wales', *The Nationalist*, (March 1909), 8-13.

'THE GREATEST EVENT IN THE ANNALS OF WALES'

[1] Rankin, op.cit., 101.

[2] NLW MSS O.M. Edwards Papers AG5/3/132.

[3] Rhoscomyl, *Flame-Bearers of Welsh History* (1905, Public Edition), v-vii.

[4] ibid.

[5] *Wales*, (ed., O.M. Edwards), (1895), 55.

[6] Huw Walters, *'Syr John Mewn Print'*, *Y Casglwr*, 10 (Mawrth 1980), 11-12.

[7] Owen Rhoscomyl, op.cit., (1905, Public Edition), vii-viii.

[8] *Cymru*, 57 (Rhag. 1919), 169.

[9] ibid., 19 (1900), 104.

[10] *Cymru*, 44-45 (1913), 322; Rhoscomyl Papers, no.44.

11 J.E. Lloyd, MA, *Outlines of the History of Wales. For the use of Schools and Colleges* (Caernarvon, 1906). In his 'Preface' L.D. Jones emphasized that Lloyd had eschewed legends and traditions, adhering 'strictly to the facts of history as far as they can be ascertained from the most authentic sources . . .'; Owen Rhoscomyl, 'Gerald the Cymro', *The Nationalist*, Oct. 1908, 7.

12 Rhoscomyl, *Flame-Bearers of Welsh History* (1905: Public Edition), xv.

13 'Introduction' to the *Book of the Words*, v-ix.

14 ibid., viii.

15 WM, 23 July 1909 6; 24 July 1909, 9; *Y Genedl Gymreig*, 27 Gorff. [July] 1909.

16 WM, 24 July 1909, 9.

17 ibid.

18 ibid., 10 Aug. 1909, 5.

19 ibid., 5 Aug. 1909, 5.

20 24 July 1909, 9; WM, 22 June 1909, 4; 24 June 1909, 4.

21 ibid.

22 ibid.

23 ibid.

24 WM, 24 July 1909, 8.

25 ibid., 28 July 1909, 5; ibid., 30 July 1909, 5.

26 *Western Mail Pageant Pictures* (=WMPP), 2. (Supplement undated.)

27 WM, 27 July 1909, 8. 'How the Pageant is Dressed.'

28 ibid.

29 *Book of the Words*, 6-7.

30 ibid., 8-11; SWDN, 27 July 1909,10.

31 WMPP, 2.

32 WM, 27 July 1909, 8.

33 *Book of the Words*, 12-17; WMPP, 2.

34 *Book of the Words*, 13-15; WMPP, 2.

35 *Book of the Words*, 15-17.

36 E.A. Morphy, op.cit., 'Some Performers in the Pageant – The Legacy of Tegaingl' (unpaginated).

37 *Book of the Words*, 18-21.

38 ibid., 20-1: WMPP, 2; WM, 27 July 1909, 8.

39 *Book of the Words*, 22-7; E.A. Morphy, op.cit., 'Scenes of the Pageant' (unpaginated).

40 *Book of the Words*, 22-3.

41 *ibid., 24-5.*

42 ibid., 30.

43 WMPP, 3.

44 SWDN, 10 Aug. 1909, 6.

45 *Book of the Words*, 31-2; WM, 27 July 1909, 8.

46 *Book of the Words*, 32-3.

47 SWDN, 27 July 1909, 10.

48 *Book of the Words*, 34-5; WM, 27 July 1909, 8.

[49] *Book of the Words*, 35; WMPP, 3.

[50] ibid., 35-6; WM, 27 July 1909, 8

[51] *Book of the Words*, 37-8; WM, 27 July 1909, 8.

[52] *Book of the Words*, 39-42.

[53] WM, 27 July 1909, 8; *The Times*, 4 Feb. 1909, 11.

[54] WMPP, 3; E.A. Morphy, op.cit., 'Some Performers in the Pageant' (unpaginated).

[55] SWDN, 27 July 1909, 10; WM, 30 July 1909, 5: The 'Ivor Bach scene' proved particularly popular with the audiences at the Cardiff, Newport and Swansea Empires, 'an anticipatory exclamation of pleasure' following the announcement that it was about to be screened.

[56] *Book of the Words*, 43-4; WM, 27 July 1909, 8; E.A. Morphy, op.cit., 'Some Performers in the Pageant' (unpaginated).

[57] *Book of the Words*, 44; *The Nationalist*, (Oct. 1909), 57; WM, 31 July 1909, 8; SWDN, 27 July 1909, 11.

[58] ibid; *The Times*, 27 July 1909, 13; E.A. Morphy, op.cit., 'Scenes of the Pageant' (unpaginated).

[59] *Book of the Words*, 46-7.

[60] E.A. Morphy, op.cit., 'Some Performers in the Pageant', 'Scenes of the Pageant' (unpaginated); WM, 27 July 1909, 8.

[61] WMPP, 3.

[62] *Book of the Words*, 48-52; Rhoscomyl, *Flame-Bearers of Welsh History* (1905: School Edition), 228.

[63] WM, 27 July 1909, 8; *Book of the Words*, 65.

[64] ibid., 53; WM, 27 July 1909, 8.

[65] *Book of the Words*, 54-5.

[66] ibid., 55-6.

[67] ibid., 65.

[68] WMPP,4.

[69] E.A. Morphy, op.cit., 'Closing Scene' (unpaginated); WMPP, 4.

[70] ibid; WM, 28 July 1909, 5; SWDN, 9 Aug. 1909, 6.

REVIEW

[1] SWDN, 27 July 1909, 6.

[2] WM, 27 July 1909, 4; ibid., 6.

[3] ibid.

[4] SWDN, 9 Aug. 1909, 4.

[5] CTSWWN, 14 Aug. 909. 6.

[6] ibid.

[7] SWDN, 9 Aug. 1909, 6; ibid., 10 Aug. 1909, 6. WM, 31 July 1909, 8.

[8] *The Sphere* (Supplement), 31 July 1909, i-iv.

[9] *The Times*, 27 July 1909, 13.

[10] SWDN, 2 Aug. 1909, 4, 6; WM, 7 Aug. 1909, 7.
[11] SWDN, 9 Aug. 1909, 5, 6; *The Nationalist*, III (Oct.1909), 57.
[12] ibid., 8-15.
[13] ibid., 14.
[14] ibid., (March 1909), 8-13.
[15] J. Glyn Davies Papers.
[16] ibid.; SWDN, 9 Aug. 1909, 5; ibid., 11 Aug. 1909, 6.
[17] *The Times*, 4 Feb. 1909, 11. WM, 24 July 1909, 9.
[18] *The Nationalist*, (March 1909), 12; ibid., (Oct. 1909) 2-3; CTSWWN, 14 Aug. 1909, 6.
[19] WM, 3 Nov.1909, 4; ibid., 9 Nov. 1909, 6; SWDN, 6 Nov. 1909., 6.
[20] WM, 26 Oct. 1909, 6; ibid., 27 Oct. 1909, 6; ibid., 9 Nov. 1909, 6.
[21] WM, 9 Nov. 1909, 6.
[22] *The Nationalist*, Oct. 1909, 15.
[23] *The Cambrian*, 20 Aug. 1909, 4; J. Glyn Davies Papers.
[24] *The Times*, 13 Dec. 1910, 11.
[25] *Book of the Words*, iii.
[26] *The Welsh Outlook*, VI (1919), 272.
[27] *The Times*, 26 July 1909, 10; Angela Gaffney, '"A National Valhalla for Wales": D.A. Thomas and the Welsh Historical Sculpture Scheme', *Transactions of the Honourable Society of Cymmrodorion*, 5 (1999), 131-44; WM, 12 Aug. 1913, 4.
[28] Rhoscomyl, *Flame-Bearers of Welsh History*, 209.
[29] WM, 5 Feb. 1909, 5; ibid., 24 July 1909, 9. It should be noted that following a preliminary edition, a further three editions of the *Book of the Words* appeared in 1909 without any structural differences between them. 'Llywelyn Olav' and Glyndŵr remained fixed in Interlude 4.
[30] WM, 26 Oct. 1909, 7.
[31] WM, 23 July 1909, 5; ibid., 14 Dec. 1909, 6.
[32] ibid.
[33] Owen Rhoscomyl, *The Book of the Investiture* (Cardiff, 1911), 16.
[34] *The Evening Standard* was quoted in WM, 24 July 1909, 9.
[35] SWDN, 2 Aug. 1909, 4, 6-7. See John S. Ellis, 'The Prince and the Dragon: Welsh National Identity and the 1911 Investiture of The Prince of Wales', *Welsh History Review*, 18, 2 (Dec. 1996), 290-1.
[36] *Y Brython*, 29 Gorff. 1909, 2.
[37] *Y Geninen*, xxvii (Hyd.1909) 68-72.
[38] WM, 18 June 1909, 4, 6; ibid., 16 June 1909, 4-5; ibid., 17 June 1909, 4-5.
[39] Steve Attridge, *Nationalism, Imperialism and Identity in Late Victorian Culture* (Palgrave Macmillan, 2003), 164, 172-3, 177.
[40] Owen Rhoscomyl Papers, no. 20; WM, 4 Feb. 1909, 9.
[41] *The Manchester Guardian*, 22 Feb.1909, 14.
[42] SWDN, 3 Aug. 1909, 5.
[43] ibid.

[44] WM, 31 July 1909, 8. W. Llewelyn Williams (1867-1922), a history graduate of Brasenose College, Oxford was in his time a journalist, barrister, Liberal MP for Carmarthen boroughs, author, eisteddfod zealot and a campaigner for a self-governing Wales within the United Kingdom. E.T. John (1857-1931), a man of Glamorgan, industrialist and Liberal MP for east Denbighshire, 1910-18, was a firm believer in a self-governing Wales and a crusader for the Welsh language.

[45] ibid.

[46] WM, 11 Aug. 1909, 6.

[47] J.F. Rees, *The Problems of Wales and Other Essays* (Cardiff, 1963), 16.

[48] Information kindly provided by Mr A.R. Allan of Liverpool University; WM, 4 Feb. 1909, 6; Rhoscomyl Papers, no.44.

[49] *The Manchester Guardian*, 22 Feb. 1909, 14; *The Western Mail*, 18 Oct. 1919, in noting what Wales had lost in his death, emphasized his 'remarkable knowledge of Welsh history' and his unremitting efforts to create an atmosphere of loyalty to Wales as a nation.' His books, journalism and lectures had 'forced Welsh Nationalists to acknowledge in him a man of arresting ability whose original views on the historic past were the outcome of close study untrammelled by conventionality or the influence of any particular school.' For that there was a price to pay: 'Those acquainted with Welsh life are not surprised that he met with numerous critics [who were obviously loath to venture into print], but to-day there remains the unanimous verdict that Rhoscomyl served his country well and gave her student-sons much food for reflection during their researches into her past.' Post-1919 Wales, however, would show little evidence that it shared *The Weekly Mail's* evaluation of Rhoscomyl's legacy.

[50] Rhoscomyl, 'The Place of Wales in the Empire', 369-71; idem., WM, 13 July 1911.

[51] John S. Ellis, 'Reconciling the Celt: British National Identity, Empire, and the 1911 Investiture of the Prince of Wales', *Journal of British Studies*, 37 (Oct. 1998) 413.

[52] Owen Rhoscomyl, 'The Place of Wales in the Empire', 370.

[53] *The Nationalist*, (May 1908), 19.

[54] WM, 18 June 1909, 4; ibid., 17 June 1909, 4.

[55] WM, 27 July 1909, 4; ibid., 7 Aug. 1909, 6.

[56] *Cofnodion a Chyfansoddiadau Eisteddfod Genedlaethol 1912 (Gwrecsam)*, 170-72.